DAILY INSPIRATION FOR EVERYDAY MEN

A COLLECTION OF 365
INSPIRATIONAL QUOTES

Published 2024 by **FiNGER**PRINT!
An imprint of Prakash Books India Pvt. Ltd

113/A, Darya Ganj,
New Delhi-110 002
Email: info@prakashbooks.com/sales@prakashbooks.com

Fingerprint Publishing
@FingerprintP
@fingerprintpublishingbooks
www.fingerprintpublishing.com

DAILY INSPIRATION FOR EVERYDAY MEN
COPYRIGHT © 2011 By The Napoleon Hill Foundation

All rights reserved. No part of this publication may be reproduced, stored in a retrieval system or transmitted in any form or by any means, electronic, mechanical, photocopying, recording or otherwise (except for mentions in reviews or edited excerpts in the media) without the written permission of the publisher.

ISBN: 978 93 9018 348 7

A COLLECTION OF 365
INSPIRATIONAL QUOTES

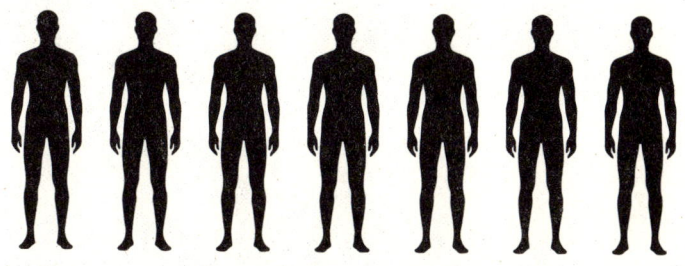

DAILY INSPIRATION FOR EVERYDAY MEN

NAPOLEON HILL
DON M. GREEN

Introduction

Are you serious about success? If so, use this inspirational calendar to serve and remind you daily of your personal commitment to achieve your goals and lifelong purpose.

Designed for men, this inspirational tool enables you to focus on one or two of Dr. Hill's Success Principles per month. Brief descriptions of the 17 success principles align with the daily quotations.

Use this perpetual calendar to jumpstart your journey. As you set short-term and long-term goals for yourself, you will begin to see why many people turn to Dr. Hill for guidance and reassurance as they begin their personal quest toward success.

Good thoughts produce good outcomes. What you think about you become. Think on these quotations daily and set your sights on success. You will be surprised at how much you can achieve when you fine tune your focus and ready your aim.

Positively,

Don M. Green

Definiteness of Purpose

Definiteness of Purpose is the starting point of all achievement. All individual achievement begins with the adoption of a definite major purpose and a specific plan for its attainment. Without a purpose and a plan, people drift aimlessly throughout life. Lack of Definiteness of Purpose is the greatest stumbling block to 98 out of every 100 persons because they never really define their goals and start toward them with Definiteness of Purpose. Ideas form the foundation of all fortunes and the starting point of all inventions. Once a student learns how to harness the power of his mind and then how to organize the knowledge, he begins to keep his mind on the things he wants and off the things he does not want.

True wealth comes from living a purposeful life and money is a means to an end, not the end.

— *Richard J. Krasney*

January 1

Dream lofty dreams and as you dream,
so shall you become.

— *James Allen*

The starting point of all personal achievement is
the adoption of a Definite Major Purpose and a
definite plan for its attainment.

— *Napoleon Hill*

January 2

Patience and perseverance have a magical
effect before which difficulties disappear
and obstacles vanish.

— *John Quincy Adams*

Definiteness of Purpose develops: self-reliance,
personal initiative, imagination, enthusiasm,
self-discipline, and concentration of effort.

— *Napoleon Hill*

January 3

The last of the human freedoms—to choose
one's attitude in any given set of circumstances,
to choose one's own way.

— *Victor Frankl*

Definiteness of Purpose encourages you to
specialize in success.

— *Napoleon Hill*

January 4

Time is the only thing every person has in
precisely the same quantity.

— *David Brinkley*

Definiteness of Purpose encourages budgeting
of time and money so efforts remain focused on
attaining your Definite Major Purpose.

— *Napoleon Hill*

January 5

What we learn to do, we learn by doing.
— *Aristotle*

Definiteness of Purpose alerts the mind to opportunities and gives courage for action.
— *Napoleon Hill*

January 6

At the day of judgment we shall not be asked what we have read but what we have done.
— *Thomas A. Kempis*

Definiteness of Purpose helps develop the capacity to reach decisions.

— *Napoleon Hill*

January 7

I don't like that man; I'm going to have to get to know him better.

— *Abraham Lincoln*

Definiteness of Purpose inspires the cooperation of others.

— *Napoleon Hill*

January 8

I'm a firm believer in luck, and I've found the harder I work, the luckier I get.

— *Thomas Jefferson*

Definiteness of Purpose prepares the mind for faith.

— *Napoleon Hill*

January 9

Just as a picture is drawn by an artist,
surroundings are created by the activities
of the mind.

— *Buddha*

Definiteness of Purpose provides a
success consciousness.

— *Napoleon Hill*

January 10

I know of no more encouraging fact than the
unquestionable ability of man to elevate his life
by a conscious endeavor.

— *Henry David Thoreau*

All individual achievements are the result of a
motive or a combination of motives. There are
nine basic motives inspiring all voluntary action.

— *Napoleon Hill*

January 11

The grand essentials to happiness in this life
are something to do, something to love,
and something to hope for.

— *Joseph Addison*

Motive One:
—the emotion of love (greatest of all motives).
— *Napoleon Hill*

January 12

You can make more friends in two months by
becoming interested in other people than you
can in two years by trying to get other people
interested in you.

— *Dale Carnegie*

Motive Two:
—the emotion of sex.

— *Napoleon Hill*

January 13

Nothing succeeds like excess.

— *Oscar Wilde*

Motive Three:
—the desire for material gain.

— *Napoleon Hill*

January 14

Let us endeavor so to live that when we come to
die even the undertaker will be sorry.

— *Mark Twain*

Motive Four:
—the desire for self-preservation.

— *Napoleon Hill*

January 15

Men are only as great as they are kind.
— *Elbert Hubbard*

Motive Five:
—the desire for freedom of body and mind.
— *Napoleon Hill*

January 16

The greatest thing in the world is to know how to be one's own self.
— *Michel de Montaigne*

Motive Six:
—the desire for self-expression and recognition.
— *Napoleon Hill*

JANUARY 17

Our reach must exceed our grasp.

— *Oswald Chambers*

Motive Seven:
—the desire for life after death.

— *Napoleon Hill*

JANUARY 18

We did not weave the web of life—we are merely a strand in it. Whatever we do to the web, we do to ourselves.

— *Chief Seattle*

Motive Eight:
—the desire for revenge.

— *Napoleon Hill*

January 19

In the middle of difficulty lies opportunity.
— *Albert Einstein*

Motive Nine:
—the emotion of fear.

— *Napoleon Hill*

January 20

Very often it happens that a discovery is made
whilst working upon quite another problem.
— *Thomas Alva Edison*

Any dominating idea, plan or purpose held in
the mind through repetition of thought and
emotionalized with a burning desire for its
realization, is taken over by the subconscious
mind and acted upon through whatever natural
and logical means may be available.

— *Napoleon Hill*

January 21

Any fact facing us is not as important as our attitude toward it, for that determines our success or failure.

— *Norman Vincent Peale*

Conscious Mind
- reasoning/thinking faculty
- deliberates, analyzes
- selects Definite Major Purpose
- guardian of subconscious

Subconscious Mind
- natural, uncultivated mind responds instinctively to emotion
- develops the power of will

— *Napoleon Hill*

January 22

Though I do not believe that a plant will spring up where no seed has been, I have great faith in a seed. Convince me that you have a seed there, and I am prepared to expect wonders.

— *Henry David Thoreau*

Any dominating desire, plan or purpose which is backed by faith is taken over by the subconscious mind.

— *Napoleon Hill*

January 23

As knowledge increases, wonder deepens.
— *Charles Morgan*

Creative genius lies within the power of the subconscious mind.
— *Napoleon Hill*

January 24

When schemes are laid in advance, it is surprising how often the circumstances fit in with them.
— *Sir William Osler*

The nine factors responsible for developing creative genius are: Definiteness of Purpose, Applied Faith, Enthusiasm, Imagination, Motive, Personal Initiative, Habit of Going the Extra Mile, Master Mind Alliance, and Positive Mental Attitude.
— *Napoleon Hill*

January 25

To achieve what you want, you must want enough to achieve.

— *Walter M. Germain*

The power of thought is the only thing over which any human being has complete, unquestionable control.

— *Napoleon Hill*

January 26

As soon as you trust yourself, you will know how to live.

— *Goethe*

The subconscious mind appears to be the only doorway of individual approach to Infinite Intelligence, and it is capable of being influenced by the individual.

— *Napoleon Hill*

JANUARY 27

An idea is salvation by imagination.

— Frank Lloyd Wright

Every brain is both a broadcasting station and a receiving set for the vibrations of thought—a fact which explains the importance of moving with Definiteness of Purpose instead of drifting along in life—since the brain may be so charged with definiteness of purpose that it will begin to attract the physical appearance of that purpose.

— Napoleon Hill

JANUARY 28

The miracle is this—the more we share, the more we have.

— Leonard Nimoy

Nothing can be achieved unless one is willing to give something in return.

— Napoleon Hill

January 29

Any jackass can kick down a barn, but it takes a carpenter to build one.
— *Sam Rayburn*

Write out a clear, concise plan by which you intend to achieve your definite major purpose. Keep this plan to yourself, except for members of your Master Mind Alliance.
— *Napoleon Hill*

January 30

It is no use waking anywhere to preach unless our walking is our preaching.
— *St. Francis of Assisi*

Keep your mind on the things you want and off the things you do not want.
— *Napoleon Hill*

January 31

Adversity introduces a person to himself.

— *Epictetus*

Remember: Your only limitation is that which you set up in your own mind by your neglect in keeping your mental attitude positive.

— *Napoleon Hill*

Master Mind
Alliance

The Master Mind Alliance principle consists of an alliance of two or more minds working together in perfect harmony for the attainment of a definite objective. Success does not come without the cooperation of others. The Master Mind Alliance principle is a practical medium through which you may appropriate and use the full benefits of the experience, training, education, specialized knowledge, and native intelligence of others as completely as if it were your own. An active alliance of two or more minds, in a spirit of perfect harmony for the attainment of a common objective, stimulates each mind to a higher degree of courage than that ordinarily experienced, and paves the way for the state of mind known as Faith.

I believe that this mastermind principle begins inside each of us. We are all two people: a positive person and a negative person.

— *Raymond Campbell*

February 1

Successful people in this world are those who get up and look for circumstances they want. If they can't find them, they make them.
— *George Bernard Shaw*

The Master Mind principle consists of an alliance of two or more minds working in perfect harmony for the attainment of a definite objective.
— *Napoleon Hill*

February 2

My best friend is the one who brings out the best in me.
— *Henry Ford*

The Master Mind principle is a practical medium through which you may appropriate and use the full benefits of the experience, the training, the education, the specialized knowledge and native intelligence of other people, as completely as if they were your own.
— *Napoleon Hill*

February 3

Nothing splendid has ever been achieved except by those who dared believe that something inside them was superior to circumstance.

— *Bruce Barton*

An active alliance of two or more minds in a spirit of perfect harmony for the attainment of a common objective, stimulates each mind to a higher degree of courage than that ordinarily experienced, and paves the way for that state of mind known as faith.

— *Napoleon Hill*

February 4

Responsibility is the thing people dread most of all. Yet it is the one thing in the world that develops us, gives us manhood or womanhood fiber.

— *Frank Crane*

Once a Master Mind Alliance is formed, the group as a whole must become and remain active.

— *Napoleon Hill*

February 5

To be prepared is half the victory.

— *Cervantes*

The group must move on a definite plan,
at a definite time, toward a definite
common objective.

— *Napoleon Hill*

February 6

A person who doubts himself is like a man who
would enlist in the ranks of his enemies.

— *Alexandre Dumas*

There must be a complete meeting of the minds.
Discord is not permitted.

— *Napoleon Hill*

February 7

Our aspirations are our possibilities.

— *Robert Browning*

A Master Mind Alliance, properly conducted, stimulates each mind in the alliance to move with enthusiasm, personal initiative, and imagination and accelerates the capacity of the minds in the alliance to receive and transmit thought vibrations through telepathy and the sixth sense.

— *Napoleon Hill*

February 8

As we let our own light shine, we unconsciously give other people permission to do the same.

— *Nelson Mandela*

The Master Mind principle, when actively applied, has the effect of connecting the subconscious sections of the minds of the allies, and gives each member full access to the spiritual powers of all the other members.

— *Napoleon Hill*

February 9

The great pleasure in life is doing what people say you cannot do.

— *Walter Bagehot*

It is a matter of established record that all individual successes, based upon any kind of achievement above mediocrity, are attained through the Master Mind principle.

— *Napoleon Hill*

February 10

Your opinion of others is apt to be their opinion of you.

— *B. C. Forbes*

One type of Master Mind is for purely social or personal reasons, consisting of one's relatives, friends and religious advisers, where no material gain is sought.

— *Napoleon Hill*

February 11

Everything is easy after someone shows you how.

— *Christopher Columbus*

The other type of Master Mind is the occupational, business or professional alliance, consisting of individuals who have a motive of a material or financial nature; in other words, an economic alliance, designed to help you sell your personal services, your skill, your ability, or to help you succeed in business.

— *Napoleon Hill*

February 12

Too many people miss the silver lining because they're expecting gold.

— *Maurice Setter*

There are Twelve Great Riches that individuals aspire to in life. They are: a positive mental attitude, sound physical health, harmony in human relationships, freedom from fear, the hope of achievement, the capacity for faith, willingness to share one's blessings, a labor of love, an open mind on all subjects, self-discipline, the capacity to understand people, and financial security.

— *Napoleon Hill*

February 13

It's hard to beat a person who never gives up.
— *Babe Ruth*

Step 1: Adopt a Definite Purpose as an objective to be attained by the alliance choosing individual members whose education, experience, and influence are such as to make them of the greatest value in achieving that purpose.
— *Napoleon Hill*

February 14

Anything in life worth having is worth working for!
— *Andrew Carnegie*

Step 2: Determine what appropriate benefit each member may receive in return for his cooperation in the alliance.
— *Napoleon Hill*

February 15

When love and skill work together,
expect a masterpiece.

— *John Ruskin*

Step 3: Establish a definite place where the members of the alliance will meet, have a definite plan, and arrange a definite time for the mutual discussion of the plan.

— *Napoleon Hill*

February 16

To will is to select a goal, determine a course of action that will bring one to that goal, and then hold to that action till the goal is reached. The key is action.

— *Michael Hanson*

Step 4: It is the burden of the leader of the alliance to see that harmony among all the members is maintained and that action is continuous in the pursuance of the Definite Major Objective.

— *Napoleon Hill*

February 17

Heaven never helps the man who will not act.
— *Sophocles*

Step 5: The watchword of the alliance should be Definiteness of Purpose, Positiveness of Plan, backed by continuous perfect harmony.
— *Napoleon Hill*

February 18

Responsibility is the price of greatness.
— *Winston Churchill*

Step 6: The number of individuals in an alliance should be governed entirely by the nature and magnitude of the purpose to be attained.
— *Napoleon Hill*

February 19

Be good at what you're good at.

— *Thomas Moore*

Begin at once to establish a true Master Mind Alliance. Select individuals you accept and who accept you. Do not choose someone just because you like him.

— *Napoleon Hill*

February 20

Life is a mirror and will reflect back to the thinker what he thinks into it.

— *Ernest Holmes*

When the members of your alliance have been selected, take them into your absolute confidence regarding your purposes and plans.

— *Napoleon Hill*

February 21

Impossible is a word to be found only in the dictionary of fools.

— *Napoleon Bonaparte*

Don't tell any one else of the alliance. Reveal your desires and plans only to the members of your Master Mind Alliance.

— *Napoleon Hill*

February 22

All that is necessary for the triumph of evil is that good men do nothing.

— *Edmund Burke*

Work out a schedule for contacting each other frequently.

— *Napoleon Hill*

February 23

All things are difficult before they are easy.
— *Thomas Fuller*

At each meeting have a report of your individual
and collective progress toward the goal.
— *Napoleon Hill*

February 24

We cannot always oblige, but we can
always speak obligingly.
— *Voltaire*

At the first sign of any lack of harmony among
the members, find out what is causing it.
— *Napoleon Hill*

February 25

It is better to correct your own faults than those of another.
— *Democritus*

If the negative attitude of any particular member is causing the lack of harmony, deal with the problem at once.
— *Napoleon Hill*

February 26

Facing it—always facing it—that's the way to get through! Face it!
— *Joseph Conrad*

If required, remove the negative member from the group. Otherwise, convert the member to the principles of this philosophy.
— *Napoleon Hill*

February 27

If the only prayer you ever say in your life is
thank you, it will be enough.

— *Meister Eckart*

Keep your mind positive and receptive at all
times. Especially when you appear before your
Master Mind group.

— *Napoleon Hill*

February 28

You cannot dream yourself into a character; you
must hammer and forge yourself one.

— *James A. Froude*

Get on good terms with yourself as you
work to develop a successful Master Mind
Alliance with others.

— *Napoleon Hill*

Applied Faith

Faith is an active state of mind. This belief in yourself is applied to achieving a definite major purpose in life. Faith is an abstract idea, a purely mental concept. Faith is the activity of individual minds facing themselves and establishing a working association with Infinite Intelligence. When a plan comes through to your conscious mind while you are open to the guidance of Infinite Intelligence, accept it with appreciation and gratitude and act on it at once. Do not hesitate, do not argue, challenge, worry, fret about it, or wonder if it's right. Act on it! Action is the first requirement of all faith. As the Bible states: "Faith without works is dead."

Through Applied Faith, I followed my instincts and found my way to the principles that inevitably would change my life.

— *Emiliano Vitale*

March 1

The idea is to seek a vision that gives you
purpose in life and then to implement
that vision.

— *Lewis P. Johnson*

Faith is a state of mind which you may develop
by conditioning your mind to receive Infinite
Intelligence.

— *Napoleon Hill*

March 2

But what is happiness except the simple harmony
between a man and the life he leads?

— *Albert Camus*

Applied faith is adapting the power
received from Infinite Intelligence to a
Definite Major Purpose.

— *Napoleon Hill*

March 3

Begin, be bold, and venture to be wise.

— *Horace*

Faith is the state of mind in which you contact the power of Infinite Intelligence and focus it upon the object of your desire.

— *Napoleon Hill*

March 4

Sometimes the best gain is to lose.

— *George Herbert*

Faith is a state of mind wherein you temporarily relax your reason and will power, and open your mind completely to the guidance of Infinite Intelligence for the attainment of some definite purpose.

— *Napoleon Hill*

March 5

Never let the odds keep you from pursuing
what you know in your heart you were
meant to do.

— *Satchel Paige*

The guidance comes in the form of an idea or
plan which comes to you while you are in this
receptive attitude.

— *Napoleon Hill*

March 6

In the province of mind, what one believes to
be true either is true or becomes true.

— *John Lilly*

The subconscious mind is the gateway between
our conscious mind and the vast reservoir of
Infinite Intelligence.

— *Napoleon Hill*

March 7

The real voyage of discovery consists not in seeking new landscapes but in having new eyes.

— *Marcel Proust*

The power of Infinite Intelligence pours life into us as a flowing stream, maintaining all of the functions of our bodies and minds, and we can use it to guide and govern the circumstances and conditions of our lives, if we will act as conductors of this energy and shape it according to our constructive purposes.

— *Napoleon Hill*

March 8

No one would ever have crossed the ocean if he could have gotten off the ship in the storm.

— *Charles Kettering*

If you would have faith—keep your mind on that which you want and off that which you do not want.

— *Napoleon Hill*

March 9

Your vision will become clear only when you can look into your heart. Who looks outside, dreams; who looks inside, awakes.

— *Carl Jung*

Steps to Faith:
- Express a definite desire for the achievement of a purpose and relate it to one or more of the basic motives.
- Create a definite and specific plan for the attainment of that desire.
- Start acting on that plan, putting every conscious effort behind it.

— *Napoleon Hill*

March 10

Great things are not done by impulse, but by a series of small things brought together.

— *Vincent Van Gogh*

When the plan comes through to your conscious mind, accept it with appreciation and gratitude and act on it at once!

— *Napoleon Hill*

March 11

God gives every bird food, but He does not
throw it into the nest.

— *J. G. Holland*

Accept with gratitude a plan by means of
which you can fulfill your desires through
the rule of hard work backed by a
burning desire.

— *Napoleon Hill*

March 12

Satisfaction isn't so much getting what you want
as wanting what you have.

— *David G. Myers*

You must give an equivalent value for the object
of your desires!

— *Napoleon Hill*

March 13

Do all the good you can, in all the ways you can,
as long as ever you can.

— *John Wesley*

When you pray, make your prayer an expression
of gratitude and thanksgiving for the blessings
you have already received.

— *Napoleon Hill*

March 14

Pessimism never won any battle.

— *Dwight D. Eisenhower*

To succeed in life you must rid yourself of the
negative influences of fear before faith can
come into your mind.

— *Napoleon Hill*

March 15

Riches get their value from the mind of their possessor; they are blessings to those who know how to use them, curses to those who do not.

— *Terence*

Fear of poverty is the most destructive of fears and also the most difficult to master.

— *Napoleon Hill*

March 16

I will allow no man to belittle my soul by making me hate him.

— *Booker T. Washington*

Fear of criticism is almost as general as the fear of poverty.

— *Napoleon Hill*

March 17

To know the laws that govern the winds, and to know that you know them, will give you an easy mind on your voyage round the world; otherwise, you may tremble at the appearance of every cloud.

— *Joshua Slocum*

Fear of ill health is related to the fear of death. There is overwhelming evidence that a disease can originate as a negative thought which the person continues to sell to himself until through auto-suggestion physical symptoms actually appear.

— *Napoleon Hill*

March 18

It's a funny thing about life; if you refuse to accept anything but the best, you very often get it.

— *W. Somerset Maugham*

Most doctors now agree that there is a definite relationship between the patient's mental attitude and his physical condition.

— *Napoleon Hill*

March 19

Man never made any material as resilient
as the human spirit.

— *Bern Williams*

You can guarantee yourself sound physical health
by maintaining a positive mental attitude and
developing a sound health consciousness whereby
you expect, demand and receive health-sustaining
elements from your food, the fresh air and sunshine!

— *Napoleon Hill*

March 20

A marriage is like a long trip in a tiny rowboat:
If one passenger starts to rock the boat, the
other has to steady it; otherwise, they will go to
the bottom together.

— *David Reuben*

Fear of the loss of love is the basis of jealousy
and overly-dependent relationships.

— *Napoleon Hill*

March 21

Life is too short to be little.

— *Benjamin Disraeli*

Fear of old age is related to a person's need to be needed.

— *Napoleon Hill*

March 22

No man is wise enough by himself.

— *Plautus*

Fear of loss of liberty is related to a person's need to feel independent and autonomous.

— *Napoleon Hill*

March 23

If you deliberately plan to be less than you
are capable of being, then I warn you that you
will be unhappy for the rest of your life.
You'll be evading your own capacities,
your own possibilities.

— *Dr. Abraham Maslow*

Fear of death is a universal fear and seems
related to a person's need to feel a sense of
worth validated by continued life.

— *Napoleon Hill*

March 24

Let your hook always be cast; in the pool where
you least expect it, there will be a fish.

— *Ovid*

The mind attracts to it the counterpart of
that which it dwells upon.

— *Napoleon Hill*

March 25

There are risks and costs to a program of action,
but they are far less than the long range risks
and costs of comfortable inactions.

— *John F. Kennedy*

Before the state of mind known as faith will
produce practical results, it must be expressed in
some form of action.

— *Napoleon Hill*

March 26

Fear is lack of faith. Lack of faith is ignorance.
Fear can only be cured by vision.

— *Horace Traubel*

Faith is the act of believing by doing.

— *Napoleon Hill*

March 27

A great deal of talent is lost in the world for want of a little courage.
— *Sydney Smith*

One of the greatest things you can do with applied faith is to refuse to think about things you do not want and feed your mind on the things you do want until you start getting them.
— *Napoleon Hill*

March 28

By the work one knows the workman.
— *Jean de La Fontaine*

Faith without works is dead.
— *Napoleon Hill*

March 29

I will love the light, for it shows me the way,
yet I will endure the darkness for it
shows me the stars.

— *Og Mandino*

Faith can give you the strength to move through temporary defeat.

— *Napoleon Hill*

March 30

There is but one cause of human failure and that is man's lack of faith in his true Self.

— *William James*

Faith can tune you into the possibilities existing even within defeat.

— *Napoleon Hill*

March 31

The lowest ebb is the turn of the tide.
— *Henry Wadsworth Longfellow*

Faith can help you discover that every adversity carries with it the seed of an equivalent or greater benefit.

— *Napoleon Hill*

Going the Extra Mile

Going the Extra Mile is the action of rendering more and better service than that for which you are presently paid. When you Go The Extra Mile, the Law of Compensation comes into play. This Universal Law neither permits any living thing to get something for nothing nor allows any form of labor to go unrewarded. You will find that Mother Nature goes the extra mile in everything that she does. She doesn't create just barely enough of each gene or species to get by; she produces an over abundance to take care of all emergencies that arise and still have enough left to guarantee the perpetuation of each form of life.

Incorporating the philosophy of going the extra mile into your work ethic is one of the best ways to insure that you will come out on top in even the most competitive business or work environments.

— *Eliezer A. Alperstein*

April 1

The World is a great mirror. It reflects
back to you what you are.

— *Thomas Drier*

Going the Extra Mile places the Law of
Increasing Returns at your command and
working for your benefit.

— *Napoleon Hill*

April 2

Whenever I hear, "It can't be done,"
I know I'm close to success.

— *Michael Flatley*

The habit of doing more than that for which
you are being paid causes you to benefit by the
Law of Compensation through which no act
or deed will or can be expressed without an
equivalent reaction after its own kind.

— *Napoleon Hill*

April 3

A great leader never sets himself above his
followers except in carrying responsibilities.

— *Jules Ormont*

You must render the greatest amount of service
of which you are capable and render it in a
friendly, positive manner.

— *Napoleon Hill*

April 4

If your actions inspire others to dream more,
learn more, do more and become more,
you are a leader.

— *John Quincy Adams*

You must do this regardless of your immediate
compensation—even if it appears that you will
receive no immediate compensation whatsoever!

— *Napoleon Hill*

April 5

All the beautiful sentiments in the world weigh
less than a simple lovely action.

— *James Russell Lowell*

Until a man begins to render more service than
that for which he is paid, he is not entitled to
more pay than he receives for that service, since,
obviously, he is already receiving full pay for
what he does!

— *Napoleon Hill*

April 6

Start by doing what's necessary,
then what's possible and suddenly you
are doing the impossible.

— *St. Francis of Assisi*

98 out of 100 wage earners have no Definite
Purpose greater than that of working for a daily
wage. Therefore, no matter how much work
they do, or how well they do it, the "wheel of
fortune" turns past them without giving them
more than a bare living, because they neither
expect nor demand more!

— *Napoleon Hill*

April 7

You must respect the things in life that
you want to attract.

— *Mike Murdock*

The habit of doing more than you are paid for
will bring you to the favorable attention of those
who have opportunities to offer.

— *Napoleon Hill*

April 8

No man is more than another unless he
does more than another.

— *Cervantes*

You will never command more than average
compensation until you become indispensable
to somebody or some group.

— *Napoleon Hill*

April 9

The highest reward for man's toil is not what he gets for it, but what he becomes by it.
— *John Ruskin*

Going the Extra Mile leads to your mental growth and physical perfection in various forms of service, thereby developing a greater ability and skill in your chosen vocation.
— *Napoleon Hill*

April 10

It is better to contract yourself within the compass of a small fortune and be happy, than to have a great one and be wretched.
— *Epictetus*

Going the Extra Mile protects you against the loss of employment and places you in a position to choose your own job and working conditions.
— *Napoleon Hill*

April 11

We build too many walls and not
enough bridges.

— *Sir Isaac Newton*

Going the Extra Mile turns the spotlight on
you and gives you the benefit of the Law of
Contrast, which is very important
in advertising yourself.

— *Napoleon Hill*

April 12

When a thing is thoroughly well done it often
has the air of being a miracle.

— *Arnold Bennett*

Doing more than you are immediately paid for
leads to the development of a positive, pleasing
attitude, which is among the more important
traits of a Pleasing Personality.

— *Napoleon Hill*

April 13

The real source of wealth is in our minds, and those of us with the richest ideas will create the greatest wealth in the world.
— *Paul McKenna*

Going the Extra Mile definitely gives you greater confidence in yourself and puts you on a better basis with your own conscience.
— *Napoleon Hill*

April 14

A man cannot directly choose his circumstances, but he can choose his thoughts, and so indirectly, yet surely, shape his circumstances.
— *James Allen*

Going the Extra Mile aids one in overcoming the destructive habit of procrastination.
— *Napoleon Hill*

April 15

Not to decide is to decide.

— *Harvey Cox*

Going the Extra Mile helps you develop
Definiteness of Purpose, without which one
cannot hope for success.

— *Napoleon Hill*

April 16

Far and away the best prize that life offers
is the chance to work hard at work
worth doing.

— *Theodore Roosevelt*

If you never do anything more than you get paid
for, you'll never get paid for anything more than
you do.

— *Napoleon Hill*

April 17

Real joy comes not from ease or riches or from the praise of men, but from doing something worth while.

— *Sir Wilfred Grenfell*

The habit of Going the Extra Mile is one which you may adopt and follow on your own initiative without asking the permission of anyone to do so.

— *Napoleon Hill*

April 18

Each of us is given a heritage and a legacy the moment we come into this world: talents, time, life. What we do with these possessions, how we invest them, determines what we are.

— *Marcus Bach*

Quality of service rendered + Quantity of service rendered + the Mental Attitude in which it is rendered = your compensation.

— *Napoleon Hill*

April 19

Throughout life we hardly realize that we receive a great deal more than we give. It is only with gratitude that life becomes rich.

— *Dietrich Bonhoeffer*

$Q^1 + Q^2 + MA = $ Compensation

— *Napoleon Hill*

April 20

A man should never be ashamed to own he has been in the wrong which is by saying in other words, that he is wiser today than he was yesterday.

— *Alexander Pope*

Each time you perform an act with the attitude that you are going to excel all of your previous achievements you are really growing.

— *Napoleon Hill*

April 21

If people knew how hard I have had to
work to gain my mastery, it would not
seem wonderful at all.

— *Michelangelo*

Going the Extra Mile is one way of writing
yourself an insurance policy against the fear of
poverty, fear of want, and against the low pay
competition of the "clock watcher."

— *Napoleon Hill*

April 22

A successful individual typically sets his next
goal somewhat but not too much
above his last achievement. In this way he
steadily raises his level of aspiration.

— *Kurt Lewin*

Going the Extra Mile turns the spotlight on
you and gives you the benefit of the Law of
Contrast, a good way to advertise yourself.

— *Napoleon Hill*

April 23

Underpromise; overdeliver.

— *Tom Peters*

The habit of rendering more and better service than you are immediately compensated for develops the habit of Personal Initiative.

— *Napoleon Hill*

April 24

In putting off what one has to do, one runs the risk of never being able to do it.

— *Charles Baudelaire*

Personal Initiative means doing the thing that needs to be done without somebody telling you to do it.

— *Napoleon Hill*

April 25

When your will is ready, your feet are light.
— *George Herbert*

Don't wait for things to happen,
make them happen.
— *Napoleon Hill*

April 26

And above all things, never think that you're
not good enough yourself. A man should never
think that. My belief is that in life people will
take you at your own reckoning.
— *Anthony Trollope*

You know, sometimes the hardest guy in the
world to get along with is the one walking
around under your own hat.
— *Napoleon Hill*

April 27

It is the soul and not the strong-box,
which should be filled.

— *Seneca*

It pays to be on good terms with your
own conscious.

— *Napoleon Hill*

April 28

Motivation is when your dreams put on
work clothes.

— *Benjamin Franklin*

You must do what you are paid for, to keep the
job, but you have the privilege of rendering an
overplus of service as a means of accumulating a
reserve credit of goodwill which entitles you to
higher pay and a better position.

— *Napoleon Hill*

April 29

He who is false to the present duty breaks a
thread in the loom, and you will see the effect
when the weaving of a lifetime is unraveled.
— *William Ellery Channing*

If the type of service you are trained to render
does not bring the compensation
you feel that you require, then possibly you
should consider a change of occupation.
— *Napoleon Hill*

April 30

Upon deciding, be quick to act.
— *Maximilien Robespierre*

The habit of Going the Extra Mile is one
which you may adopt and follow on your own
initiative, without asking the permission of
anyone to do so.
— *Napoleon Hill*

Pleasing Personality

Personality is the sum total of one's mental, spiritual, and physical traits and habits that distinguish one from all others. It is the factor that determines whether one is liked or disliked by others. Your personality is your greatest asset or liability. It embraces everything you control—mind, body and soul. Some characteristics of a pleasing personality include: positive mental attitude, flexibility, sincerity, prompt actions, courtesy, tactfulness, pleasing tone of voice, smile, and tolerance.

All that is needed to develop a pleasing personality is a sincere heart, genuine love for others, and an appreciation for the differences that may exist between you and others.

— *Stephen Grant*

May 1

The spirit of self-help is the root of all genuine growth in the individual.

— *Samuel Smiles*

Every person achieving a high degree of personal success has mastered the art of successfully selling himself.

— *Napoleon Hill*

May 2

We either make ourselves miserable,
or we make ourselves strong.
The amount of work is the same.

— *Carlos Castaneda*

Persons possessing a pleasing personality attract success. They turn on others.
Sour souls, know-it-alls, and negative persons only attract failure and they are real turn-offs.

— *Napoleon Hill*

May 3

Self-love, my liege, is not so vile a sin as self-neglect.

— *William Shakespeare*

A Positive Mental Attitude heads the list as the most important trait necessary in developing a Pleasing Personality. Positive is more than merely the opposite of negative. It means having assurance, confidence, a belief in self, a feeling of rightness, and a belief in one's capacity to achieve one's Definite Major Purpose.

— *Napoleon Hill*

May 4

Use what talent you possess: the woods would be very silent if no birds sang except those that sang best.

— *Henry Van Dyke*

Flexibility consists in the habit of adapting one's self to quickly changing circumstances without losing one's sense of composure or confidence.

— *Napoleon Hill*

May 5

You don't have to blow out the other fellow's
light to let your own shine.

— *Bernard M. Baruch*

Courtesy is the habit of rendering useful service
without the expectation of direct reward, the
habit of respecting other people's feelings under
all circumstances, the habit of going out of one's
way if need be to help any less fortunate person
whenever possible, and last, but not least, the
habit of controlling selfishness, and greed, and
envy, and hatred.

— *Napoleon Hill*

May 6

And thou wilt give thyself relief, if thou doest
every act of thy life as if it were the last.

— *Marcus Aurelius*

People who like people are usually liked by
others. People who dislike others generally are
not liked by others.

— *Napoleon Hill*

May 7

There is a destiny that makes us brothers
    no one goes his way alone;
  all that we send into the lives of others,
    comes back into our own.

— Edwin Markham

The Habit of Smiling is directly related to a
Positive Mental Attitude. It's a reflection of faith
and joy. If you do not possess this trait, you
should begin immediately practicing before a
mirror. Smiling and success go together hand
in hand.

— Napoleon Hill

May 8

The greatest of faults is to be conscious
of none.

— Thomas Carlyle

Tolerance consists of an open mind on all
subjects, toward all people, at all times.
In addition to being one of the more important
of the traits of a pleasing personality, an open
mind on all subjects is one of the Twelve Great
Riches of Life.

— Napoleon Hill

May 9

Flatter me, and I may not believe you.
   Criticize me, and I may not like you.
   Ignore me, and I may not forgive you.
   Encourage me, and I will not forget you.
— *William Arthur Ward*

Tactfulness consists in doing and saying the right thing at the right time.
— *Napoleon Hill*

May 10

Don't judge each day by the harvest you reap, but by the seeds you plant.
—*Robert Louis Stevenson*

Sincerity begins with you. The man who is sincere with others must first be sincere with himself.

— *Napoleon Hill*

May 11

How far you go in life depends on your being tender with the young, compassionate with the aged, sympathetic with the striving, and tolerant of the weak and strong because someday in your life, you will have been all of these.
— *George Washington*

While we have no tails to wag, our face, with its many muscles and numerous possible shapes, serves as a mirror of one's self, reflecting the inner man. As such, the smile, the tone of voice, and the expression of the face constitute open windows through which others may see our inner selves.
— *Napoleon Hill*

May 12

The way to gain a good reputation is to be what you desire to appear.
— *Socrates*

Men of sound character always have the courage to deal directly and openly with others and they follow this habit even though it may at times be to their disadvantage. However, honesty yields fewer regrets than dishonesty, and it creates a soundness of mind and spirit which comes through the practice of maintaining a clear conscience.
— *Napoleon Hill*

May 13

Try not to become a man of success.
Rather become a man of value.

— *Albert Einstein*

Humility of the heart is a sign of great inner
strength and confidence.

— *Napoleon Hill*

May 14

Common sense . . . is very uncommon.

— *Lord Chesterfield*

Watch your tongue. It has no mind of its own.
Keep it within your cheek and keep your brain
in charge of your mouth.

— *Napoleon Hill*

May 15

We lift ourselves by our thought, we climb upon
our vision of ourselves.

— *Orison Swett Marden*

Life, from birth until death, is dependent to a
large degree upon salesmanship.

— *Napoleon Hill*

May 16

All higher humor begins with ceasing to
take oneself seriously.

— *Hermann Hesse*

Humor is a sign of faith and is the product of
a Positive Mental Attitude. Humor guards one
against being overcome by fear and failure. It
gives a bounce to life and the human spirit.

— *Napoleon Hill*

Personal Initiative

"There are two types of men," said Andrew Carnegie, "who never amount to anything. One is the fellow who never does anything except that which he is told to do, the other is the fellow who never does more than he is told to do. The man who gets ahead does the thing that should be done without being told to do it, but he does not stop there, he goes the extra mile by doing a great deal more than is expected or demanded of him." Personal Initiative is the power that inspires the completion of that which one begins. It is the power that starts all action. No person is free until he learns to do his own thinking and gains the courage to act on his own Personal Initiative—it is the twin brother of Going the Extra Mile.

Personal initiative is the ability to do it now. It is the ability to create your own plan and execute the plan, without having been told what to do. Do it now.

— *Fred Wikkeling*

May 17

Our main business is not to see what lies
dimly at a distance, but to do what lies
clearly at hand.

— *Thomas Carlyle*

Personal Initiative bears the same relationship to an
individual that a self-starter bears to an automobile.
It is the power that inspires the completion of that
which one begins. There are many starters among
men, but there are few finishers.

— *Napoleon Hill*

May 18

Nothing is so difficult that it may not be
won by industry.

— *Terence*

Personal Initiative reveals favorable
opportunities for self-advancement and inspires
one to embrace them and realize
their full potential.

— *Napoleon Hill*

May 19

Half the things that people do not succeed in
are through fear of making the attempt.

— *James Northcote*

Men with Personal Initiative do not drift
aimlessly, but sail boldly out across the
seas of personal success.

— *Napoleon Hill*

May 20

The chief way to gain good will is by
good deeds.

— *Cicero*

Therefore, if you would be done with the negative
side of the street then prepare yourself to cross
over and begin walking down the avenue named
Positive. Move on your Personal Initiative.

— *Napoleon Hill*

May 21

A purpose is the eternal condition
of success.

— *Theodore T. Munger*

The mind that has been made ready to
receive attracts that which it needs, just as an
electromagnet attracts steel filings.

— *Napoleon Hill*

May 22

Chiefly the mould of a man's fortune is in
his own hands.

—*Francis Bacon*

The most difficult part of any task is that of
making a start at performing it.

— *Napoleon Hill*

May 23

In the long run, men hit only what they aim at.
Therefore . . . they had better aim at
something high.

— *Henry David Thoreau*

Winners are those persons who get in the game
and dare to compete for the prize of
life's great riches.

— *Napoleon Hill*

May 24

It thou believest a thing impossible, thy
despondency shall make it so; but he that
persevereth, shall overcome all difficulties.

— *Philip Dormer Stanhope*

There is always the tendency to wait for a better
day or for that moment described as when the
"time is right." However, once a start has been
made, the power of performance presents itself.

— *Napoleon Hill*

May 25

Great things are done when men and mountains meet.

— *William Blake*

Adopt a Definite Major Purpose and see how quickly the habit of moving on your own Personal Initiative will inspire you to action in carrying out the object of your purpose.

— *Napoleon Hill*

May 26

Never despair. But if you do, work on in despair.

— *Edmund Burke*

In conclusion, it should be pointed out once more that few games are ever won by players sitting on the sidelines. If you want to win at life you then must get involved.

— *Napoleon Hill*

Personal Initiative

May 27

Genius is eternal patience.

— *Michelangelo*

You must be willing to pay the price of success, and that usually can be translated into such terms as: sweat and strain, tears and toil, hope and hurt, brains and brawn.

— *Napoleon Hill*

May 28

It is wonderful what we can do if we're always doing.

— *George Washington*

Success is reserved for those persons who are dedicated to the proposition that achievers are doers and that success comes to those who are about the business of succeeding in life.

— *Napoleon Hill*

May 29

A nail is driven out by another nail, habit
is overcome by habit.

— *Erasmus*

Somewhere along the way you will meet your
"other self" face to face—that which can and
will carry you over onto the successful side of
the street.

— *Napoleon Hill*

May 30

You can preach a better sermon with your life
than with your lips.

— *Oliver Goldsmith*

Never mind how much you know. The
important thing is what you can do with
what you know!

— *Napoleon Hill*

May 31

There is no fate that plans men's lives. Whatever comes to us, good or bad, is usually the result of our own action or lack of action.

—*Herbert N. Casson*

Winners are self-starters. They are action-oriented, always taking the initiative. They do not wait on success, but are continually moving in the direction of realizing life goals.

— *Napoleon Hill*

Positive Mental Attitude

Positive Mental Attitude is the right mental attitude in all circumstances. Keep your mind on the things you want and off the things you don't want. Remember the old French proverb: "Be very careful what you set your heart on, for you will surely achieve it." Success attracts more success while failure attracts more failure. This principle presents the means by which the entire philosophy can best be assimilated and put to practical use. You cannot get the most out of the other sixteen principles without understanding and applying this one.

I've seen how living life with a positive mental attitude backed with applied faith can help a person deal with despair, anguish, and great pain and infect the multitudes in a good way.

— Phil Barlow

June 1

Such as are your habitual thoughts, such also
will be the character of your mind; for the soul
is dyed by the color of the thoughts.
— *Marcus Aurelius*

Thoughts are powerful.
— *Napoleon Hill*

June 2

Let the mind be a thoroughfare for all thoughts.
— *John Keats*

Ideas can capture the human spirit, move the
masses, and turn an entire society about face.
— *Napoleon Hill*

June 3

Our acts make or mar us; we are the children of our own deeds.

— *Victor Hugo*

Remember: "As a man thinketh in his heart, so is he."

— *Napoleon Hill*

June 4

The men who do the most with their lives are those who approach human existence, its opportunities and its problems—even in rough moments—with a confident attitude and an enthusiastic point of view.

— *Norman Vincent Peale*

Any man who takes himself seriously and dares to think the thoughts of personal growth and gain must add the creative catalyst of a Positive Mental Attitude.

— *Napoleon Hill*

June 5

The greatest revolution of our generation is the discovery that human beings, by changing the inner attitudes of their minds, can change the outer aspect of their lives.

— *William James*

An attitude can be described as a psychological posture.

— *Napoleon Hill*

June 6

There is nothing that makes men rich and strong but that which they carry inside of them. Wealth is of the heart, not of the hand.

— *John Milton*

Self-actualization is an important concept. Actualization means the transformation of possibilities into realities.
Self-actualization means reaching deep within yourself and bringing forth your very best efforts.

— *Napoleon Hill*

June 7

Chances are right now you are standing in the middle of your own acre of diamonds.

— *Earl Nightingale*

Behind the concept and reality of self-actualization is a belief in the goodness of "rightness" of life. This is a positive statement and affirms that everyone has a place in life and a right to live life at the fullest.

— *Napoleon Hill*

June 8

Every now and then a man's mind is stretched by a new idea and never shrinks back to its original proportions.

— *Oliver Wendell Holmes*

Remember: Thoughts shape our lives!

— *Napoleon Hill*

June 9

A rock pile ceases to be a rock pile the moment
a single man contemplates it, bearing within him
the image of a cathedral.

— *Antoine de Saint-Exupery*

You can take possession of your thought power
or you can let it be influenced by all the stray
winds of chance and undesirable circumstances.

— *Napoleon Hill*

June 10

The stronger the winds, the deeper the roots,
and the longer the winds, the more
beautiful the tree.

— *Charles Swindoll*

Even in the midst of great adversity, the positive
person tells himself over and over again that life
is good and he can weather the storm.

— *Napoleon Hill*

June 11

There is only one corner of the universe you can be certain of improving, and that's your own self.
— *Aldous Huxley*

The mental in Positive Mental Attitude is the dynamic of thought which provides for the continual reinforcement of the feeling of confidence and belief in one's self.
— *Napoleon Hill*

June 12

It is not the ship so much as the skilled sailing that assures the prosperous voyage.
— *George William Curtis*

The man who has a Positive Mental Attitude is one who has assumed a life posture which permits him to confidently face life situations.
— *Napoleon Hill*

June 13

We must cultivate our garden.

— *Voltaire*

Our beliefs must be continually reinforced.
The muscles of self-confidence must be
strengthened through a daily workout, mental in
design, so that in the midst of adversity one will
be strong enough to win in spite of the odds.

— *Napoleon Hill*

June 14

Sometimes our light goes out but is blown again
into flame by an encounter with another human
being. Each of us owes deepest thanks to those
who have rekindled this inner light.

— *Albert Schweitzer*

Peace of mind can only be obtained through a
Positive Mental Attitude. Peace of mind requires
helping others to help themselves.

— *Napoleon Hill*

June 15

It's a good thing to turn your mind upside
down now and then, like an hourglass, to let the
particles run the other way.
— *Christopher Morley*

A Positive Mental Attitude is the first and the
most important step we must take in the control
and direction of our minds since all degrees of
a negative mental attitude leave us wide open to
every negative influence we contact.
— *Napoleon Hill*

June 16

If a man be gracious and courteous to strangers,
it shows he is a citizen of the world, and that his
heart is no island cut off from other islands, but
a continent that joins to them.
— *Francis Bacon*

You can develop a Positive Mental
Attitude by selecting a pace-maker, and
emulating him.
— *Napoleon Hill*

June 17

God gives every bird food, but He does not throw it into the nest.

— *J. G. Holland*

It is important to realize that the great crime of the universe is stagnation.

— *Napoleon Hill*

June 18

More things are wrought by prayer than this world dreams of.

— *Lord Tennyson*

Positive Mental Attitude is the only condition of the mind in which we can express Applied Faith and draw upon the forces of Infinite Intelligence.

— *Napoleon Hill*

June 19

When your emotional nature is stirred by something you do, is it not probably that your heart is actually stimulated, so that it quickens the circulation of your blood and makes you feel alive and full of health?

— *David Dunn*

Positive Mental Attitude is the only condition which permits us to get on the Success Beam.

— *Napoleon Hill*

June 20

One of the most important results you can bring into the world is the ***you*** that you really want to be.

— *Robert Fritz*

Positive Mental Attitude is the only condition of the mind in which we can meet and recognize our "other self"—that self which has no limitations.

— *Napoleon Hill*

June 21

Most of the shadows of this life are caused by standing in our own sunshine.
— *Ralph Waldo Emerson*

Remember that no one is ever rewarded or promoted because of a bad disposition and a negative mental attitude.
— *Napoleon Hill*

June 22

If you have built castles in the air your work need not be lost; that is where they should be. Now put the foundations under them.
— *Henry David Thoreau*

To maintain the feeling of confidence, there must be repetitious thought charged with assurance and belief itself.
— *Napoleon Hill*

June 23

Where you stumble, there your treasure lies.

— *Joseph Campbell*

Individuals with positive mental attitudes
are never found in a rut.

— *Napoleon Hill*

June 24

We grow great by dreams.
All big men are dreamers.

— *Woodrow Wilson*

It is the believing man who achieves.

— *Napoleon Hill*

June 25

Holding on to anger is like grasping a hot coal
with the intent of throwing it at someone else;
you are the one who gets burned.
— *Siddhartha Gautama Buddha*

You can form the habit of tolerance and keep an
open mind on all subjects, toward people of all
races and creeds, and learn to like people as they
are instead of demanding them to be like you.
— *Napoleon Hill*

June 26

Action is the foundational key to success.
— *Pablo Picasso*

Winners are those persons in life who have
taken possession of their minds, exercise control
over their thoughts and maintain a Positive
Mental Attitude in their quest for success.
— *Napoleon Hill*

June 27

Anyone can steer the ship, but it takes a leader
to chart the course.

— *John Maxwell*

You can take possession of your thought power
or you can let it be influenced by all the stray
winds of chance and undesirable circumstances.

— *Napoleon Hill*

June 28

Virtue, like art, constantly deals with what is
hard to do; and the harder the task, the better
the success.

— *Aristotle*

A Positive Mental Attitude is generated when
a person assumes a confident life-stance which
originates and is sustained through the control
of one's thoughts.

— *Napoleon Hill*

June 29

Whatever you have, you must either use or lose.
— *Henry Ford*

Keep your mind on the things you want and off the things you don't want. Remember the old French proverb: "Be very careful what you set your heart on, for you will surely achieve it."
— *Napoleon Hill*

June 30

When I was a boy of fourteen, my father was so ignorant I could hardly stand to have the old man around. But when I got to be twenty-one, I was astonished at how much he had learned in seven years.
— *Mark Twain*

Adjust yourself to other people's states of mind and their peculiarities so as to get along peacefully with them, and refrain from taking notice of trivial circumstances in your human relations by refusing to allow them to become controversial incidents.
— *Napoleon Hill*

Enthusiasm

Enthusiasm is faith in action. Enthusiasm comes from the Greek words "en" which means "in" and "theos" which means "God." It is the intense emotion known as burning desire. Enthusiasm comes from within, although it radiates outwardly in the expression of one's voice and countenance. Enthusiasm is power because it is the instrument by which adversities and failures and temporary defeats may be transmuted into action backed by faith. The flame of enthusiasm burning within you turns thought into action.

Believe in yourself, and the world will believe in you!

— *Jim Oleson*

July 1

All that we need to make us really happy is something to be enthusiastic about.
— *Charles Kingsley*

Enthusiasm causes one to glow with self-confidence.
— *Napoleon Hill*

July 2

Every man is enthusiastic at times. One man has enthusiasm for thirty minutes—another man has it for thirty days, but it is the man who has it for thirty years who makes a success in life.
— *Edward B. Butler*

Enthusiasm definitely takes the drudgery out of labor.
— *Napoleon Hill*

July 3

Those who attempt to search into the majesty of
God will be overwhelmed with its glory.

— *Thomas à Kempis*

Enthusiasm is the utilization of the God
within you and the ability to tap and direct this
tremendous force.

— *Napoleon Hill*

July 4

For the conduct of life, habits are more
important than maxims because a habit is a
maxim verified. To take a new set of maxims
for one's guide is no more than to change the
title of a book, but to change one's habits is to
change one's life. Life is only a tissue of habits.

— *Frederic Amiel*

Remember, you are developing the habit of
Controlled Enthusiasm and the creation
of habits requires repetition through
physical action.

— *Napoleon Hill*

July 5

The more we do, the more we can do.
— *William Hazlitt*

Enthusiasm steps up thought vibrations and stimulates the imagination.
— *Napoleon Hill*

July 6

Experience shows that success is due less to ability than to zeal. The winner is he who gives himself to his work, body and soul.
— *Charles Buxton*

Enthusiasm gives a thrust to life, an impetus toward success.
— *Napoleon Hill*

July 7

The most powerful weapon on earth is the human soul on fire.

— *Marshal Foch*

Enthusiasm concentrates the powers of the mind and gives them the wings of action.

— *Napoleon Hill*

July 8

Kind words do not cost much. They never blister the tongue nor lips. Mental trouble was never known to arise from such quarters. Though they do not cost much, yet they accomplish much. They make other people good-natured. They also produce their own image on men's souls, and a beautiful image it is.

— *Pascal*

Enthusiasm gives brilliance and color to the spoken word.

— *Napoleon Hill*

July 9

Enthusiasm finds the opportunities and energy makes the most of them.
— *Henry S. Haskins*

Enthusiasm is power, because it is the instrument by which adversities and failures and temporary defeat may be transmuted into action backed by faith.
— *Napoleon Hill*

July 10

Opportunity, sooner or later, comes to all who work and wish.
— *Lord Stanley*

Enthusiasm is "faith in action," pushing aside those obstacles which stand between a man and his Definite Major Purpose.
— *Napoleon Hill*

July 11

If at times we are somewhat stunned by the
tempest, never fear. Let us take breath,
and go on afresh.

— *St. Francis de Sales*

Enthusiasm moves mountains, blows apart negative
thoughts, repels the negativism of others, secures
support for your ideas, enlists the cooperation of
others, encourages confidence, and underscores
your sincerity of purpose.

— *Napoleon Hill*

July 12

Our greatest happiness does not depend on the
condition of life in which chance has placed us,
but is always the result of a good conscience, good
health, occupation, and freedom in all just pursuits.

— *Thomas Jefferson*

Give a man a burning desire to achieve a definite
end, and a definite motive setting fire to that desire
and very quickly the flames of enthusiasm will
begin burning and a power will be generated which,
when properly directed, will assist a person in
realizing their Definite Major Purpose.

— *Napoleon Hill*

July 13

Faith is the daring of the soul to go farther than it can see.

— *William Newton Clark*

Enthusiasm clears the mind of negative cobwebs and prepares the way for the "faith in action" so vital to personal success.

— *Napoleon Hill*

July 14

You will become as small as your controlling desire; as great as your dominant aspiration.

— *James Allen*

Remember, enthusiasm thrives on a positive spirit.

— *Napoleon Hill*

July 15

Face each day cheerfully, smilingly and
courageously, and it will naturally follow that
your work will be a real pleasure, and progress
with be a delightful accomplishment.

— *William M. Peck*

Enthusiasm is the "action factor of thought!"
Where it is strong enough, it literally forces
one into action appropriate to the nature of the
motive which inspired it.

— *Napoleon Hill*

Teamwork

Teamwork is harmonious cooperation that is willing, voluntary and free. Whenever the spirit of Teamwork is the dominating influence in business or industry, success is inevitable. Harmonious cooperation is a priceless asset that you can acquire in proportion to your giving. Teamwork, in a spirit of friendliness, costs little in the way of time and effort. Generosity, fair treatment, courtesy, and a willingness to serve are qualities that pay high dividends whenever they are applied in human relations.

Teamwork divides the task and doubles the success.

— Frank Kirk

July 16

If a man does not make new acquaintances as he advances through life he will soon find himself left alone. A man . . . should keep his friendships in constant repair.

— *Samuel Johnson*

Cooperation, like love and friendship, is something one receives by giving.

— *Napoleon Hill*

July 17

If I wanted to become a failure, I would seek advice from men who have never succeeded. If I wanted to succeed in all things, I would look around me for those who are succeeding, and do as they have done.

— *Joseph Marshall Wade*

Underdogs can become winners when they believe themselves capable of winning and are willing to commit themselves to victory.

— *Napoleon Hill*

July 18

To the being fully alive, the future is not ominous but a promise; it surrounds the present like a halo.

— *John Dewey*

Not only does your present and future depend upon your ability to join hands with others— but the tomorrow our children will know will depend upon how willing we are to walk the road of life together in peace and prosperity as we build a better world.

— *Napoleon Hill*

July 19

The weakest among us has a gift, however seemingly trivial, which is peculiar to him and which, worthily used, will be a gift also to his race.

— *John Ruskin*

The cooperative spirit is a gift which can be offered to another human being.

— *Napoleon Hill*

July 20

We are the miracle of miracles, the great inscrutable mystery of God.

— *Thomas Carlyle*

The cooperative spirit is also a torch which can be passed on to another generation, holding high the light of hope and love, peace and prosperity.

— *Napoleon Hill*

July 21

A community cannot be happy in one part and unhappy in another. It's all or nothing, no patching any more for ever.

— *H. G. Wells*

A cooperative spirit increases your success potential while benefiting others.

— *Napoleon Hill*

Teamwork

July 22

Human brotherhood is not just a goal. It is a condition on which our way of life depends. The question for our time is not whether all men are bothers. That question has been answered by the God who placed us on this earth together. The question is whether we have the strength and the will to make the brotherhood of man the guiding principle of our daily lives.

— *John F. Kennedy*

We are not only surrounded by the water of humanity, but we are connected and joined together by common concerns, interests and needs which bind us and create the very ground of our being and the human experience.

— *Napoleon Hill*

July 23

The Duke of Wellington is reported to have said, "The British are not braver than the French—they are only brave for five minutes longer."
Courage consists not in blindly overlooking danger, but in seeing it and conquering it.

— *Jean Paul Richter*

A contagious enthusiasm is required if a group is to become "fired-up" and prepared for victory.

— *Napoleon Hill*

July 24

The empires of the future are the empires
of the mind.

— *Winston Churchill*

Winners win because they believe
winning possible.

— *Napoleon Hill*

July 25

The quality of a man's life is in direct proportion
to his commitment to excellence, regardless of
his chosen field of endeavor.

— *Vince Lombardi*

Willing teamwork is the only type that leads to
constructive ends, the only type that sustains the
power of people through coordinated efforts.

— *Napoleon Hill*

July 26

If it is not in the interest of the public it is not in the interest of business.

— *Joseph H. Defrees*

Teamwork produces power, but the question as to whether the power is temporary or permanent depends upon the motive that inspires the cooperation.

— *Napoleon Hill*

July 27

Two men working as a team will produce more than three men working as individuals.

— *Charles P. McCormick*

Victory, if it is to be realized, requires team effort—teamwork.

— *Napoleon Hill*

July 28

The most precious thing anyone—man or store, anybody or anything—can have is the goodwill of others. It is something as fragile as an orchid. And as beautiful! As precious as a gold nugget—and as hard to find.

— *Amos Parrish*

The individual attempting to win at life or the organization attempting to realize great gains needs to understand the reality of momentum.

— *Napoleon Hill*

July 29

I do not believe in a fate that falls on men however they act, but I do believe in a fate that falls on them unless they act.

— *G. K. Chesterton*

In the life of every man or any organization, there are times when an added power is needed to carry on through seeming failure to the point of victory.

— *Napoleon Hill*

July 30

Either I will find a way, or I will make one.

— *Sir Philip Sidney*

Great physical power can be produced by coordination of efforts but the endurance of that power—its quality, scope, and strength are taken from that intangible something known as the "spirit" in which people work together for the attainment of a common goal.

— *Napoleon Hill*

July 31

When moral courage feels that it is in the right, there is no personal daring of which it is incapable.

— *Leigh Hunt*

It's a wise man who understands that there is strength in numbers and integrity through unity.

— *Napoleon Hill*

Self-Discipline

Self-Discipline means taking possession of your own mind. Self-Discipline begins with the mastery of thought. If you do not control your thoughts, you cannot control your needs. Self-Discipline calls for a balancing of the emotions of your heart with the reasoning faculty of your head. It is the bottleneck through which all of your personal power for success must flow. Direct your thoughts, control your emotions, and ordain your destiny. As our culture has become more complex, the need for self-control has increased.

Self-Discipline is the way you pay forward your future success or failure by your thoughts and actions today, and every day.

— *Tom Cunningham*

August 1

The talent of success is nothing more than
doing what you can do well; and doing well
whatever you do, without a thought of fame.
— *Henry Wadsworth Longfellow*

People who keep on winning in life are those
who are willing to pay the price of success
in terms of developing and maintaining
constructive, success-producing habits.
— *Napoleon Hill*

August 2

I am only one, but I am one. I cannot do
everything, but I can do something. And I will
not let what I cannot do interfere with
what I can do.
— *Edward Everett Hale*

Self-discipline means taking possession of your
own mind.
— *Napoleon Hill*

August 3

One of the chief reasons for success in life is the ability to maintain a daily interest in one's work, to have a chronic enthusiasm, to regard each day as important.

— *William Lyon Phelps*

What you are as a person, whether it be success or failure, depends to a large degree upon your personal habits.

— *Napoleon Hill*

August 4

Success begins with a fellow's will. It's all in the state of mind.

— *Walter D. Wintle*

You can choose to create within you habits that are success-producing.

— *Napoleon Hill*

August 5

Dreams are the seedlings of realities.

— *James Allen*

The most important habits are those which have to do with the thoughts you think.

— *Napoleon Hill*

August 6

Life is the faculty of spontaneous activity, the awareness that we have powers.

— *Immanuel Kant*

It doesn't take too long to realize that what a man thinks is translated into physical terms with regard to what he does and achieves in life.

— *Napoleon Hill*

August 7

Screw your courage to the sticking-place,
And we'll not fail.

— *William Shakespeare*

When you have gained control over your thought habits, you will have come a long way in realizing the type of Self-Discipline that speeds up the success process.

— *Napoleon Hill*

August 8

If you wish success in life, make perseverance your bosom friend, experience your wise counselor, caution your elder brother, and hope your guardian genius.

— *Joseph Addison*

As a rule of thumb, keep your plans to yourself.

— *Napoleon Hill*

August 9

Whatever you attempt, go at it with spirit.
— *David Starr Jordan*

Shoot for the stars! It may not be in the best taste
for you to over-shoot your abilities in terms of
personal ambition, but it is a lot better than setting
an easily obtainable goal which requires little effort.
— *Napoleon Hill*

August 10

I am not bound to win but I am bound to be true. I
am not bound to succeed but I am bound to live up
to what light I have. I must stand with anybody that
stands right: stand with him while he is right and
part with him when he goes wrong.
— *Abraham Lincoln*

If you aim at a very big achievement and only
obtain a moderate achievement, you still have
realized a goal of great value.
— *Napoleon Hill*

August 11

This is the foundation of success nine times out of ten—having confidence in yourself and applying yourself with all your might to your work.

— *Thomas E. Wilson*

If you allow yourself to be held back in the beginning, you will have only sold yourself short.

— *Napoleon Hill*

August 12

No life ever grows great until it is dedicated, focused, disciplined.

— *Harry Emerson Fosdick*

Self-discipline represents the "bottleneck" through which the great power within this Science must pass.

— *Napoleon Hill*

August 13

He started to sing as he tackled the thing
That couldn't be done, and he did it.
— *Edgar A. Guest*

Self-discipline is a quality/habit you should persistently apply as it grows stronger with the passing of time and moves you ever closer to success.
— *Napoleon Hill*

August 14

There are two significant characteristics of every great life. The first is capacity to make a good beginning and the second is courage to push on to a good ending.
— *Harold B. Walker*

Adopt the motto: "Deeds not words."
Let your actions talk for you.
— *Napoleon Hill*

August 15

Public opinion is a weak tyrant compared with our own private opinion. What a man thinks of himself, that it is which determines, or rather indicates, his fate.

— *Henry David Thoreau*

You will find a lot more people willing to tear you down by discouragement than you will find flattering you and building up your ego. Of course, the best way to avoid such discouragement is to confide in no one but those who have a genuine sympathy with your cause and an understanding of life's great possibilities.

— *Napoleon Hill*

Learning from Adversity and Defeat

Every adversity carries with it the seed of an equivalent or greater benefit. Individual success usually is in exact proportion to the scope of the defeat the individual has experienced and mastered. Most so-called failures represent only a temporary defeat that may prove to be a blessing in disguise. Defeat is never the same as failure unless and until it has been accepted as such.

The adversities we go through are for our own good. They teach us and give us experience that will help us or help us help others.

— *Allen Watkins*

August 16

In every failure the wise man will find the
seed of success.

— *W. Clement Stone*

Every adversity carries with it the seed of an
equivalent or a greater benefit provided
you look for it.

— *Napoleon Hill*

August 17

It has done me good to be somewhat parched
by the heat and drenched by the rain of life.

— *Henry Wadsworth Longfellow*

Most so-called failures only represent
temporary setbacks which can prove to
be blessings in disguise.

— *Napoleon Hill*

August 18

Sweet are the uses of adversity;
Which, like the toad, ugly and venomous,
Wears yet a precious jewel in his head.

— *Shakespeare*

Men who learn from adversity discover the great
pearls of the good life.

— *Napoleon Hill*

August 19

I want to know if you've touched the center
of your own sorrow, if you've been opened by
life's betrayals, or have become shriveled and
closed from fear of further pain.

— *White Crow*

Keep in mind that defeat is but a temporary
state of affairs unless you choose to accept it
as final.

— *Napoleon Hill*

August 20

Fire is the test of gold; adversity of strong men.

— *Seneca*

If we examine the records, we shall be convinced that those men who attain success are those who have adopted the habit of accepting defeat as nothing but an urge to greater effort.

— *Napoleon Hill*

August 21

Adversity has the same effect on a man that severe training has on the pugilist—it reduces him to his fighting weight.

— *Josh Billings*

Time eventually corrects all evils, rights all wrongs for those who realize that adversity is one of the great teachers of life.

— *Napoleon Hill*

August 22

When the well is dry, we know the worth of water.

— *Benjamin Franklin*

Defeat may lead to the development of a stronger will-power, provided one accepts it as a challenge to greater effort and not as a signal to stop trying.

— *Napoleon Hill*

August 23

Self-conquest is the greatest of victories.

— *Plato*

Defeat may cause one to acquire the habit of taking self-inventory for the purpose of uncovering weaknesses responsible for the defeat.

— *Napoleon Hill*

August 24

Endure and persist; the pain will turn to
good by and by.

— *Ovid*

Learning from adversity is a part of the great
system of natural laws designed by an all-wise
Creator to protect man against his own follies,
save him from him own mistakes, and insure
him against self-destruction.

— *Napoleon Hill*

August 25

When an archer misses the mark, he turns and
looks for the fault within himself. Failure to hit
the bullseye is never the fault of the target. To
improve your aim—improve yourself.

— *Gilbert Arland*

Coming to grips with this principle could
produce a critical turning point in your life.

— *Napoleon Hill*

August 26

Ninety-nine percent of the failures come from
people who have the habit of making excuses.
— *George Washington*

The man who "fails and still fights"
usually has uncovered a source of
Creative Vision enabling him to convert
temporary defeat into permanent success.
— *Napoleon Hill*

August 27

Failure is often that early morning hour of
darkness which precedes the dawning of
the day of success.
— *Lee Mitchell Hodges*

We shall find that the individual success usually
is in exact proportion to the scope of the defeat
the individual has experienced and mastered.
— *Napoleon Hill*

August 28

We cannot change the nature of a thought or of a truth, but, we can, as it were, guide the ship by moving the helm.

— *Professor Elmer Gates*

Often defeat breaks up some negative habits one has formed, thus releasing energies for a new start through the development of more positive habits.

— *Napoleon Hill*

August 29

Experience is not what happens to a man; it is what a man does with what happens to him.

— *Aldous Huxley*

The compensating benefits of failure and defeat often cannot be seen or recognized as benefits until one looks backward at the experiences after a sufficient lapse of time.

— *Napoleon Hill*

August 30

Forget the past, for it is gone from your domain!
Forget the future, for it is beyond your reach!
Control the present! Live supremely well now!
It will whitewash the dark past, and compel the
future to be bright! This is the way of the wise.
— *Paramahansa Yogananda*

The person who can go through defeat
which crushes the finer emotions, and still
avoid having his inner soul smothered by the
experience may become a master in his
chosen field of endeavor.

— *Napoleon Hill*

August 31

Never give up! If adversity presses Providence
wisely has mingled the cup,
And the best counsel, in all your distresses,
Is the stout watchword of "Never give up."
— *Martin F. Tupper*

It is crucial to note that the turning point
at which one begins to attain success in
the higher brackets of achievement usually
is marked by some form of outstanding
defeat or failure.

— *Napoleon Hill*

Controlled Attention

Controlled Attention leads to mastery in any type of human endeavor, because it enables one to focus the powers of his mind upon the attainment of a definite objective and to keep it so directed at will. Great achievements come from minds that are at peace with themselves. Peace within one's mind is not a matter of luck, but is a priceless possession, which can be attained only by Self-Discipline based upon Controlled Attention. Concentration on one's major purpose projects a clear picture of that purpose upon the conscious mind and holds it there until it is taken over by the subconscious mind and acted upon.

I know that throughout life we are going to face challenges. Regardless of what they may be, we must keep a positive mental attitude and persist. Without persistence coupled with controlled attention, we are surrendering to mediocrity.
— *Boyd McClean*

September 1

One of the most important but one of the
most difficult things for a powerful mind
is to be its own master.

— *Joseph Addison*

The mind never remains inactive. It works
continuously, reacting to those influences which
reach it.

— *Napoleon Hill*

September 2

Anything that the human mind can conceive can
be produced ultimately.

— *David Sarnoff*

Controlled Attention is an absolute prerequisite
if one is to tap into the great reservoir of power
with Infinite Intelligence.

— *Napoleon Hill*

September 3

The inlet of a man's mind is what he learns; the outlet is what he accomplishes. If his mind is not fed by a continued supply of new ideas which he puts to work with purpose, and if there is no outlet in action, his mind becomes stagnant.

— *Jeremiah W. Jenks*

Controlled Attention is the highest form of Self-Discipline.

— *Napoleon Hill*

September 4

A great mind is one that can forget or look beyond itself.

— *William Hazlitt*

Great achievements come from minds which are at peace with themselves and to those who are at peace with others.

— *Napoleon Hill*

September 5

All over the world people are seeking peace
of mind, but there can be no peace of mind
without strength of mind.

— *Eric B. Gutkind*

The difference between Controlled Attention
and casual attention is very great. It amounts to a
difference between feeding the mind on thought
material which will produce that which one desires,
and allowing the mind through neglect to feed
upon the type of garbage that will produce that
which one most fears and least desires.

— *Napoleon Hill*

September 6

The human mind is not a deep-freeze for storage
but a forge for production; it must be supplied with
fuel, fired and properly shaped.

— *William A. Donaghy*

Controlled Attention, when it is focused upon
the object of one's Definite Major Purpose,
is the medium by which one makes positive
application of the principle and process of
autosuggestion.

— *Napoleon Hill*

September 7

A mind once cultivated will not lie fallow for half an hour.

— *Edward Bulwer-Lytton*

Keep your mind on the things you want and off the things you don't want.

— *Napoleon Hill*

September 8

A weak mind is like a microscope, which magnifies trifling things but cannot receive great ones.

— *Lord Chesterfield*

A good example is a person whose thoughts are fixed upon failure and poverty. Through autosuggestion such thoughts as "I'm a loser" or "I'll never have anything" are transferred to the subconscious mind, fed back into the conscious mind and are expressed as actions which guarantee that the person will lose and have little in life.

— *Napoleon Hill*

September 9

The resolved mind hath no cares.

— *George Herbert*

It is obvious that when one voluntarily fixes his attention upon a Definite Major Purpose of a positive nature, and forces his mind to dwell on that purpose, that he "conditions" his mind to act upon that purpose.

— *Napoleon Hill*

September 10

The great business of man is to improve his mind, and govern his manners; all other projects and pursuits, whether in our power to compass or not, are only amusements.

— *Pliny*

Controlled Attention may be compared to a gardener who keeps his fertile garden spot cleared of weeds so that it may yield a bountiful harvest of edible foods.

— *Napoleon Hill*

September 11

The worth of the mind consisteth not in going
high, but in marching orderly.

— *Michel de Montaigne*

Controlled Attention is self-mastery of the
highest order. It reflects organized
mind-power. Actually, Controlled Attention and
Self-Discipline are so closely related that they
can be best described as "twin brothers."

— *Napoleon Hill*

September 12

A truly strong and sound mind is the mind
that can equally embrace great things
and small.

— *Samuel Johnson*

One either takes possession of his own mind
and directs it to the attainment of that which
he desires or his mind takes possession of him
and gives him whatever the circumstances of life
hand out.

— *Napoleon Hill*

September 13

Every mind is a great slumbering power until awakened by keen desire and by definite resolution to do.

— *Edgar F. Roberts*

Perhaps you can better understand how the principle of Controlled Attention works if you realize that one can control the span and object of attention by thinking of it, talking of it, eating it, drinking it, sleeping and dreaming it and thus making it a twenty-four hour obsession.

— *Napoleon Hill*

September 14

There will always be a Frontier where there is an open mind and a willing hand.

— *Charles F. Kettering*

Controlled Attention is the act of focusing the mind upon a given desire until the ways and means for its realization have been worked out and successfully put into operation.

— *Napoleon Hill*

September 15

Nothing is at last sacred but the integrity of your own mind.

— *Ralph Waldo Emerson*

Success in all the higher brackets of individual achievement is attained only by the application of thought power, properly organized and directed to definite ends.

— *Napoleon Hill*

Accurate
Thinking

The power of thought is the most dangerous or the most beneficial power available to man, depending, of course, upon how it is used. Through the power of thought man builds great empires of civilization. Through the same power other people trample down empires as if they were helpless clay. Thought is the only thing over which man has been given the complete privilege of control. The Accurate Thinker always submits his emotional desires and decisions to his head for judiciary examination before he relies upon them as being sound, for he knows that his head is more dependable than his heart. The Accurate Thinker separates facts from fiction and separates facts into two classes: important and unimportant.

For me, having a clear understanding of the facts and how they relate to and impact the resolution of any challenge or opportunity is critical to success.

— *Richard Banta*

September 16

Who supplies another with a constructive
thought has enriched him forever.
— *Alfred A. Montapert*

An accurate thinker sees both the way and
the doing of the way.
— *Napoleon Hill*

September 17

A thought is often original, though you have
uttered it a hundred times. It has come to you
over a new route, by a new and express train
of association.
— *Oliver Wendell Holmes*

Accurate thinking is a grasping for conclusion
through intuition after all of the possibilities
within a given situation have been explored.
— *Napoleon Hill*

September 18

Clear therefore thy head, and rally, and manage
thy thoughts rightly, and thou wilt save time,
and see and do thy business well; for thy
judgment will be distinct, thy mind free, and the
faculties strong and regular.

— *William Penn*

Remember, the accurate thinker is one who can
state a problem simply, clearly, and precisely.

— *Napoleon Hill*

September 19

The charm of a deed is its doing;
the charm of a life is its living; the soul of
the thing is the thought.

— *Eugene Fitch Ware*

Don't tackle a problem with a closed mind.

— *Napoleon Hill*

September 20

Think like a man of action and act like a man of thought.

— *Henri Bergson*

The accurate thinker is always concerned that the decisions reached and applied are consistent with one's life goals or Definite Major Purpose.

— *Napoleon Hill*

September 21

A man would do well to carry a pencil in his pocket, and write down the thoughts of the moment. Those that come unsought for are commonly the most valuable, and should be secured, because they seldom return.

— *Francis Bacon*

Each decision you reach, each step you take, ought to draw you closer to realizing your Definite Major Purpose.

— *Napoleon Hill*

Accurate Thinking

September 22

Thoughts lead on to purposes; purposes go forth in action; actions form habits; habits decide character; and character fixes our destiny.

— *Tryon Edwards*

Be patient. Be courageous. You can find your way out of the maze—a conclusion, a solution awaits you as an accurate thinker.

— *Napoleon Hill*

September 23

Thinking cannot be clear until it has had expression—we must write, or speak, or act our thoughts.

— *Henry Ward Beecher*

There is no substitute for precise thinking.

— *Napoleon Hill*

September 24

They are never alone that are accompanied with noble thoughts.
— *Sir Philip Sidney*

Stop trying to think out your problems alone and begin using the knowledge and experience and judgment of others.
— *Napoleon Hill*

September 25

We can't always control what happens to us. But we can control what we think about what happens ... And what we are thinking is our life at any particular moment.
— *Norman G. Shidle*

If the circumstances of your life are not to your liking, you may change them by changing your mental attitude to conform with the circumstances you desire.
— *Napoleon Hill*

September 26

Do not think that what your thoughts dwell
upon is of no matter. Your thoughts
are making you.

— *Bishop Steere*

The habit of accurate, organized thinking pays off.
There is no limit to the amount it pays when put
into intelligent action, except the mental limitations
which you set up in your own mind.

— *Napoleon Hill*

September 27

What is the hardest task in the world?
To think.

— *Ralph Waldo Emerson*

Next to life itself, the greatest miracle known to
man is the miracle of thought, and no small part
of this miracle consists in the amazing simplicity
with which so complicated a mechanism as the
brain can be operated by the power of will.

— *Napoleon Hill*

September 28

The ultimate value of life depends upon awareness and the power of contemplation rather than upon mere survival.

— *Aristotle*

There can be no fixed price on the value of organized thinking! But there is no power in thought until it is organized and directed toward a definite end and implemented by intelligent action.

— *Napoleon Hill*

September 29

There is nothing good or bad but thinking makes it so.

— *William Shakespeare*

"The first fact one must recognize," said Andrew Carnegie, "in order to become an accurate thinker, is the fact that the power with which one thinks is mental dynamite which can be organized and used constructively for the attainment of definite ends; but if not controlled and directed, it may become a mental explosive that will literally blast your hopes of achievement and lead to inevitable failure."

— *Napoleon Hill*

September 30

It is remarkable to what lengths people will go to avoid thought.

— *Thomas Edison*

The person who can accurately think through situations related to one's Definite Major Purpose is a craftsman and rises quickly to an enviable position.

— *Napoleon Hill*

Maintenance of
Sound Health

The mind and the body are so closely related that whatever one does affects the other. One does not enjoy sound health without a health consciousness. Sound health begins with a sound health consciousness, just as financial success begins with a prosperity consciousness. To maintain a health consciousness, one must think in terms of sound health, not in terms of illness and disease. As the old sayings go: "You have nothing if you do not have your health" and "If you think you're sick, you are."

Since my work is sedentary, it is even more important that I do something physical every day, whether it is walking the dogs or visiting the gym. I don't always practice what I preach, but I definitely feel better when I do.

— Chris Lake

October 1

It is part of the cure to wish to be cured.

— *Seneca*

If you think you are sick, you are.

— *Napoleon Hill*

October 2

The sound body is the product of the sound mind.

— *George Bernard Shaw*

We cannot separate the body and the mind,
for they are one.

— *Napoleon Hill*

October 3

To insure good health: Eat lightly, breathe
deeply, live moderately, cultivate cheerfulness,
and maintain an interest in life.

— *William Louden*

A change in mental attitude often aids in
the development of bodily resistance
against disease.

— *Napoleon Hill*

October 4

Measure your health by your sympathy with
morning and Spring.

— *Henry David Thoreau*

We are not only one in the sense of a mind-
body, but we are also part of the environment in
which we live.

— *Napoleon Hill*

October 5

The health of nations is more important
than the wealth of nations.

— *Will Durant*

The key to good health is a physically fit body
complemented by a Positive Mental Attitude
which is expressed as a positive approach to life.

— *Napoleon Hill*

October 6

Life is made up, not of great sacrifices or
duties, but of little things, in which smiles
and kindnesses, and small obligations, given
habitually, are what win and preserve the heart
and secure comfort.

— *Sir Humphry Davy*

Don't forget to express gratitude daily, by prayer
and affirmation, for the blessings you have.

— *Napoleon Hill*

October 7

The trouble about always trying to preserve the
health of the body is that it is so difficult to do
so without destroying the health of the mind.
— *G. K. Chesterton*

Success comes to those who are physically
and mentally fit.

— *Napoleon Hill*

October 8

Indulge yourself in pleasures only in so far as
they are necessary for the preservation of health.
— *Baruch Spinoza*

Don't neglect to play and relax regularly.
— *Napoleon Hill*

October 9

No duty is more urgent than that of
returning thanks.

— *St. Ambrose*

Go to bed praying and get up singing and notice
what a fine day's work you will do.

— *Napoleon Hill*

October 10

The diseases which destroy a man are no less
natural than the instincts which preserve him.

— *George Santayana*

Mental germs not only poison the psychological
system, but attack a person's physical
system as well.

— *Napoleon Hill*

October 11

To lose one's health renders science null, art inglorious, strength unavailing, wealth useless, and eloquence powerless.

— *Herophilus*

Eat right, think right, sleep right, and play right, and you can save the doctor's bill for your vacation money.

— *Napoleon Hill*

October 12

Man masters nature not by force but by understanding.

— *Jacob Bronowski*

Don't try to cure a headache. It's better to cure the thing that caused it.

— *Napoleon Hill*

October 13

Basic to an integrated life is a dominant ideal.
To plow a straight row one must keep his eye
on the goal rather than the plow.

— *J. M. Price*

As we are one with the world about us, so are
we one with ourselves: a mind-body. And as we
are affected by the world we live in, and in turn
affect that world, so our body influences our
mind, and in turn our mind influences our body.

— *Napoleon Hill*

October 14

All work is as seed sown; it grows and spreads,
and sows itself anew.

— *Thomas Carlyle*

The most successful person uses autosuggestion
as a medium for feeding his mind with the
thoughts of things and circumstances he desires,
including a health consciousness.

— *Napoleon Hill*

OCTOBER 15

"Just living is not enough," said the butterfly.
"One must have freedom, sunshine and a
little flower."
— *Hans Christian Anderson*

Some live to eat, others eat to live, and they live
better and longer.
— *Napoleon Hill*

Budgeting
Time and Money

People are divided into two classes: drifters and non-drifters. A non-drifter is a person who has a definite major purpose, a definite plan to attain that purpose, and is busily engaged in carrying out his plan. A drifter does no real thinking. He acts upon the thinking of others. Successful people ask themselves the following questions:
- How are you using your time?
- How much of it are you wasting, and
- How are you wasting it?
- What are you doing to stop this waste?
- Tell me how you use your spare time and how you spend your money, and I will tell you where and what you will be ten years from now.

When I decided to take time every day to read ***Think and Grow Rich***—and then actually to follow through and read it daily—I discovered a way that I could take control of my life.

— *Gus Gates*

October 16

Life is what happens while you are
making other plans.

— *John Lennon*

Yesterday is gone forever, now make the most
of today and tomorrow if you wish to
make up for lost time.

— *Napoleon Hill*

October 17

It is better to know some of the questions
than all of the answers.

— *James Thurber*

Every man needs to stop, look, listen and think.
And he should do this with regularity, with
purpose aforethought. He should take personal
inventory of himself at least once a month, to
make sure that he is getting the most out of life,
or to find out why he is not.

— *Napoleon Hill*

October 18

Life is tons of discipline.

— *Robert Frost*

Remember also that you will never be ready to receive the better things of life which you desire unless you put yourself under a strict system of self-discipline in the use of your time.

— *Napoleon Hill*

October 19

Do not let what you cannot do interfere with what you can do.

— *John Wooden*

Every man is where he is, and what he is, because of the habits he has acquired. The man who lives up to the limit of his income, or beyond it, never is a free man.

— *Napoleon Hill*

October 20

The safest way to double your money is to fold it over and put it in your pocket.
— *Kin Hubbard*

Frugality is one of the essentials of success. The habit of planned savings encourages frugality, makes it an established habit.
— *Napoleon Hill*

October 21

Contentment does not consist in heaping up more fuel, but in taking away some fire.
— *Thomas Fuller*

Self-examination requires self-discipline, courage, sincerity and a willingness to face facts. Successful men always are their own most severe critics and taskmasters. They maneuver the circumstances of their lives to their own advantage, instead of procrastinating and allowing circumstances to maneuver them into failure.
— *Napoleon Hill*

October 22

Man's real life is happy, chiefly because he is
ever expecting that it soon will be so.

— *Edgar Allan Poe*

The happiest men are those who have learned
to mix play with their work and bind the two
together with enthusiasm.

— *Napoleon Hill*

October 23

Independency may be found in comparative as
well as in absolute abundance; I mean where a
person contracts his desires within the limits of
his fortune.

— *William Shenstone*

The major purpose of a budget system is to
establish habits which force one to save a definite
percentage of his income so that eventually he may
acquire economic independence.

— *Napoleon Hill*

October 24

Success: A process of becoming who you already are.

— *Frank Potts*

Readiness calls for preparation through the conditioning of your mind to accept guidance from within.

— *Napoleon Hill*

October 25

If you believe in the Lord, He will do half the work—but the last half. He helps those who help themselves.

— *Cyrus H. K. Curtis*

The Creator gave you a brain to be used and constant access to the power of thought which flows into your brain from the great storehouse of Infinite Intelligence. What use are you making of this power?

— *Napoleon Hill*

October 26

The busy man has few idle visitors; to the
boiling pot the flies come not.

— *Benjamin Franklin*

Use your time wisely. Invest it in creating
relationships which are mutually rewarding
and harmonious.

— *Napoleon Hill*

October 27

The busier we are, the more acutely we feel
that we live.

— *Immanuel Kant*

If you wish a job done promptly and well, get a
busy man to do it.

— *Napoleon Hill*

October 28

Present fears are less than horrible imaginings.
— *William Shakespeare*

Clear your mind of all anxieties, all desires, all fears, and give your Creator an opportunity to speak to you.
— *Napoleon Hill*

October 29

The forty-four-hour week has no charm for me. I'm looking for a forty-hour day.
— *Nicholas Murray Butler*

Yes, your real boss is the person who walks around under your hat. Recognize this truth and you will have an adequate incentive to use your time effectively.
— *Napoleon Hill*

October 30

The great secret of success in life is for a man to
be ready when his opportunity comes.

— *Benjamin Disraeli*

By freeing your mind for one hour each
day you will be inviting opportunity to
reveal itself to you.

— *Napoleon Hill*

October 31

Most people should learn to tell their dollars
where to go instead of asking them
where they went.

— *Roger W. Babson*

Make your money work for you and you will not
have to work so hard for it.

— *Napoleon Hill*

Creative Vision

Creative Vision is developed by the free
and fearless use of one's imagination. Creative
Vision attains its ends by basically new ideas
and methods. It is not a miraculous quality with
which one is gifted or is not gifted at birth. It is
a quality that may be developed. It may be an
inborn quality of mind, or an acquired quality,
for it may be developed by the free and fearless
use of the faculty of imagination. Our country
needs Creative Vision now as it has never
needed it before.

For but a moment if we can believe that man
can fly, the possibility of flying becomes more
real. Only by taking time out to suspend our
disbelief can we manifest the impossible.

— Uriel Martinez

November 1

The body travels more easily than the mind, and until we have limbered up our imagination we continue to think as though we had stayed home. We have not really budged a step until we take up residence in someone else's point of view.
— *John Erskine*

Creative Vision is the capacity to envision new possibilities, dream new dreams, and tap into the vast powers of the universe which permit you to build a new tomorrow as you achieve your Definite Major Purpose.
— *Napoleon Hill*

November 2

The principal mark of genius is not perfection but originality, the opening of new frontiers.
— *Arthur Koestler*

Creative Vision is much more than simply a game of "let's try and think of a new idea."
— *Napoleon Hill*

NOVEMBER 3

A man to carry on a successful business must have imagination. He must see things as in a vision, a dream of the whole thing.

— *Charles Schwab*

A man introspects, which means he is capable of "tuning" in to his inner self.

— *Napoleon Hill*

NOVEMBER 4

Imagination lit every lamp in this country, produced every article we use, built every church, made every discovery, performed every act of kindness and progress, created more and better things for more people. It is the priceless ingredient for a better day.

— *Henry J. Taylor*

Imagination is the key to all achievement, the mainspring of all human endeavor, and the secret door leading to the inner-man.

— *Napoleon Hill*

November 5

The imagination imitates. It is the
critical spirit that creates.

— *Oscar Wilde*

Creative Vision is more tuned to the creative
spirit of the universe which expresses itself
through man.

— *Napoleon Hill*

November 6

Anybody can do anything that he imagines.

— *Henry Ford*

Creative Vision is reserved for the
sensitive, inspired, open-ended person who
enjoys life and wishes to drink from its
deepest wells.

— *Napoleon Hill*

November 7

True wisdom consists in not departing from nature but in molding our conduct according to her laws and model.

— *Seneca*

Imagination is the soil within which flowers the creative effort distinguishing winners from losers.

— *Napoleon Hill*

November 8

Faith is to believe what we do not see; and the reward of this faith is to see what we believe.

— *St. Augustine*

Creative Vision is definitely related to that state of mind known as Faith, and it is deeply significant that those who have demonstrated the greatest amount of creative vision are known to have been men with a great capacity for faith.

— *Napoleon Hill*

November 9

Originality does not consist in saying what no one has ever said before, but in saying exactly what you think yourself.
— *James Stephens*

Creative Vision is not a miraculous quality with which one is gifted or not gifted at birth.
— *Napoleon Hill*

November 10

I get the facts, I study them patiently, I apply imagination.
— *Bernard M. Baruch*

Creative Vision is a quality which may be developed.
— *Napoleon Hill*

November 11

A strong imagination begetteth opportunity.
— *Michel de Montaigne*

Creative Vision assists you in discovering who
you are, what you want from life, and what you
are willing to give in return.

— *Napoleon Hill*

November 12

In every rank, both great and small, it is
industry that supports us all.

— *John Gay*

The dare to do spirit of Creative Vision
inspires men to pioneer and experiment in
every field of endeavor.

— *Napoleon Hill*

November 13

National progress is the sum of individual industry, energy, and uprightness, as national decay is of individual idleness, selfishness, and vice.

—*Samuel Smiles*

Our country needs Creative Vision now as it has never needed it before.

— *Napoleon Hill*

November 14

Universal peace will be realized, not because man will become better, but because a new order of things, a new science, new economic necessities, will impose peace.

— *Anatole France*

Our nation has plenty of brawn and muscle—but what is needed desperately is an outpouring of Creative Vision if we are to meet the very complex demands we now face and surmount the crisis of complex international relationships upon which the peace and prosperity of the world depends.

— *Napoleon Hill*

Creative Vision

November 15

Thought works in silence; so does virtue. One
might erect statues to silence.

— *Thomas Carlyle*

Adopt the habit of the "silent hour" when you
will be still and listen for that small, still voice that
speaks from within, thus discovering the greatest of
all power, Creative Vision, the great power that can
help you achieve your Definite Major Purpose.

— *Napoleon Hill*

November 16

For success, attitude is equally as
important as ability.

— *Harry F. Banks*

The man possessing Creative Vision knows that
he succeeds only by helping others to succeed,
and he knows that it is not necessary for another
man to fail in order that he may succeed.

— *Napoleon Hill*

November 17

Too many young people itch for what they want without scratching for it.

— *Tom D. Taylor*

A man with Creative Vision knows what he desires of life and understands that life never permits anyone to get something of value for nothing without eventually having to pay more for it than it is worth.

— *Napoleon Hill*

November 18

The mightiest works have been accomplished by men who have kept their ability to dream great dreams.

— *Walter Bowie*

Creative Vision is a quality of mind belonging only to men who follow the habit of Going the Extra Mile. It recognizes no such thing as the regularity of working hours and it is not primarily concerned with monetary compensation as its highest aim is to achieve the "impossible."

— *Napoleon Hill*

November 19

Keep your eyes on the stars and your feet
on the ground.

— *Theodore Roosevelt*

The man with Creative Vision knows
where he is going.

— *Napoleon Hill*

November 20

Never take counsel of your fears.

— *Andrew Jackson*

The man with Creative Vision has no fear of
others, either those of higher or lower rank, for
he is at peace with himself and is fair and honest
in his relationships with others and himself.

— *Napoleon Hill*

November 21

A sage thing is timely silence, and better than any speech.

— *Plutarch*

You must go into the silence alone of your own free will and accord.

— *Napoleon Hill*

November 22

In the business world, everyone is paid in two coins: cash and experience. Take the experience first; the cash will come later.

— *Harold Geneen*

The man with Creative Vision produces results, not excuses.

— *Napoleon Hill*

November 23

Nothing will ever be attempted if all possible
objections must be first overcome.

— *Samuel Johnson*

Developing Creative Vision keeps a man so
busy achieving his Definite Major Purpose that
there is not time left for worry and doubt or fear
and frustration.

— *Napoleon Hill*

November 24

Vision is the art of seeing things invisible.

— *Jonathan Swift*

It is a well-known fact that any idea, plan or
purpose, that is brought into the conscious
mind repeatedly and supported by the
emotional feeling is automatically picked up
by the subconscious section of the mind and
carried out to its logical conclusion by means of
whatever practical media are at hand.

— *Napoleon Hill*

November 25

All human things do require to have an ideal in
them; to have some soul in them.

— *Thomas Carlyle*

The imagination has been described as "the
workshop of the soul wherein is shaped all plans
for individual achievement."

— *Napoleon Hill*

November 26

Life is the application of noble and
profound ideas to life.

— *Matthew Arnold*

Locked deep within the human spirit is a vast
reservoir of ideas and insights waiting to
be released.

— *Napoleon Hill*

November 27

Thinkers help other people to think, for they formulate what others are thinking. No person writes or thinks alone; thought is in the air but its expression is necessary to create a tangible spirit of the times.

— *Elbert Hubbard*

Nearly every fact or idea known to man is but a combination of older realities rearranged to create a new appearance or synthesis. This is synthetic imagination.

— *Napoleon Hill*

November 28

The life each of us lives is the life within the limits of our own thinking. To have life more abundant, we must think in the limitless terms of abundance.

— *Thomas Dreier*

The other type of imagination is Creative Imagination which has its base in the subconscious section of the mind and serves as the medium by which new facts or ideas are revealed through the faculty known as the "sixth sense."

— *Napoleon Hill*

November 29

What I enjoy is not the fruits alone, but I also enjoy the soil itself.

— *Cicero*

The soil within which great creative efforts blossom can be enriched by applying the seventeen success principles; i.e., the Science of Success.

— *Napoleon Hill*

November 30

While we ponder when to begin it becomes too late to do.

— *Quintilian*

The point can be made—"It makes little difference where a man begins."

— *Napoleon Hill*

Cosmic Habitforce

Cosmic Habitforce pertains to the universe as a whole and the laws that govern it. Cosmic Habitforce is Infinite Intelligence in operation. It is a sense of order. It takes over a habit and causes a person to act upon the habit automatically. Developing and establishing positive habits leads to peace of mind, health, and financial security. You are where you are and what you are because of your established habits and thoughts and deeds.

Once you have the ideas, you visualize them happening: listen to music and play over and over again in your mind the visualization of yourself achieving all your goals. What Dr. Hill states is absolutely true: "Whatever the mind can conceive and believe, it can achieve."

— *Carl Garwood*

December 1

You and I must not complain if our plans break down if we have done our part. That probably means that the plans of One who knows more than we do have succeeded.

— *Edward E. Hale*

The orderliness of the world gives evidence that all natural laws are under the control of a universal plan.

— *Napoleon Hill*

December 2

By choosing our habits, we determine the grooves into which Time will hear us; and these are grooves that enrich our lives and make for ease of mind, peace, happiness—achievement.

— *Frank B. Gilberth*

Cosmic Habitforce pertains to the entire universe and is the law by which the equilibrium of the universe is maintained through established patterns or habits.

— *Napoleon Hill*

December 3

Get the pattern of your life from God,
then go about your work and be yourself.

— *Phillips Brooks*

Cosmic Habitforce is Infinite Intelligence in action.
— *Napoleon Hill*

December 4

Men are not flattered by being shown that there
has been a difference of purpose between the
Almighty and them.

— *Abraham Lincoln*

Be sure to make your plan sufficiently flexible
so that you can change it any time that you are
inspired to do so . . . Infinite Intelligence may hand
you a better plan than the one you have made for
yourself for the achievement of your purpose.

— *Napoleon Hill*

December 5

Every man is his own ancestor, and every man his own heir. He devises his own future, and he inherits his own past.

— *H. F. Hedge*

Nothing is ever produced which does not bear many, or all, of the characteristics of its ancestors.

— *Napoleon Hill*

December 6

Follow your feelings and consider them to be the voice of your innermost beliefs.

— *George Sand*

If you treat hunches as foolish ideas, they will soon treat you the same way and stay away. When you have a hunch, no matter how foolish it may seem, put it down on paper. Examine it carefully, and you may find that it may be an assist from Infinite Intelligence intended to put you back on the beam, when you may have gotten off.

— *Napoleon Hill*

December 7

Within us all there are wells of thought and
dynamos of energy which are not suspected
until emergencies arrive.

— *Thomas J. Watson*

Cosmic Habitforce is the law which forces every
living creature, and every particle of matter,
to come under the dominating influence of its
environment, including the physical habits and
thought habits of mankind.

— *Napoleon Hill*

December 8

Joy is not in things; it is in us.

— *Richard Wagner*

Control your mental attitude, keep it positive
by exercising self-discipline, and thus prepare
the mental soil in which any worthwhile plan,
purpose or desire may be planted by repeated,
intense impression, with the assurance that
it will germinate, grow and find expression
ultimately in its material equivalent, through
whatever means are at hand.

— *Napoleon Hill*

December 9

There is always something for which to be thankful.

— *Charles Dickens*

Nature and the universe are organized and
ordered. This order, or reliability,
of nature simplifies life.

— *Napoleon Hill*

December 10

Without knowing what I am and why I am here,
life is impossible.

— *Leo Tolstoy*

Time, space, energy, matter and intelligence are
nature's building blocks with which she creates
all things.

— *Napoleon Hill*

December 11

The longer I live the more beautiful life becomes. If you foolishly ignore beauty, you will soon find yourself without it. Your life will be impoverished. But if you invest in beauty, it will remain with you all the days of your life.
— *Frank Lloyd Wright*

An oak tree grows from an acorn, and a pine tree grows from a pine nut. An acorn never produces a pine tree, nor does a pine nut produce an oak tree. Nothing is ever produced which does not bear many, or all, of the characteristics of its ancestors.
— *Napoleon Hill*

December 12

Science is the knowledge of consequences, and dependence of one fact upon another.
— *Thomas Hobbes*

There is nothing that is not controlled by this universal law of Cosmic Habitforce.
— *Napoleon Hill*

DECEMBER 13

Do not anticipate trouble, or worry about what may never happen. Keep in the sunlight.
— *Benjamin Franklin*

Negative thought habits attract to their creator physical manifestations corresponding to their nature as perfectly and as inevitably as nature germinates the acorn and develops it into an oak tree.
— *Napoleon Hill*

DECEMBER 14

The first peace, which is the most important, is that which comes within the soul of people when they realize their oneness with the universe and all its powers.
— *Black Elk*

As we have seen, our thought habits, our mental attitude, are the one and only things over which each individual has the right of complete control.
— *Napoleon Hill*

December 15

The winds of grace are always blowing. It is you
that must raise your sails.

— *Rabindranath Tagore*

All voluntary positive habits are the products
of will power directed toward the attainment of
definite goals.

— *Napoleon Hill*

December 16

Mind is the master power that moulds and
makes, and man is mind. And every more he
takes the tool of thought, and shaping what he
wills, brings forth a thousand joys, a thousand
ills. He thinks in secret and it comes to pass.
Environment is but a looking glass.

— *James Allen*

Men are all born equal in the sense that they
have equal access to this great principle. All
normal persons have the right to control their
thoughts and their mental attitude, and this is
the way in which this greatest of all natural laws
is made effective in individual lives.

— *Napoleon Hill*

December 17

The great art of learning is to understand but little at a time.

— *John Locke*

All big things are composed of smaller things of a related nature.

— *Napoleon Hill*

December 18

There are two ways you can live: as if nothing is a miracle; or as if everything is a miracle.

— *Albert Einstein*

Cosmic Habitforce has the capacity to impart a peculiar quality to one's habits of thought which removes obstacles and provides a power capable of surmounting barriers to success.

— *Napoleon Hill*

December 19

Seek out that particular mental attribute which
makes you feel most deeply and vitally alive,
along with which comes the inner voice which
says, "This is the real me," and when you have
found that attitude, follow it.

— *William James*

Our habits are created through repeated
thought and experience.

— *Napoleon Hill*

December 20

It is one of the most beautiful compensations
of this life that no man can sincerely try to help
another without helping himself.

— *Ralph Waldo Emerson*

Cosmic Habitforce is the comptroller of
all natural laws.

— *Napoleon Hill*

December 21

I can give you a six-word formula for success:
Think things through—then follow though.
— *Capt. Edward V. Rickenbacker*

It's a great moment in your life when you break away from your social heredity and start doing your own thinking.

— *Napoleon Hill*

December 22

I have yet to find the man, however exalted his station, who did not do better work and put forth greater effort under a spirit of approval than under a spirit of criticism.

— *Charles M. Schwab*

If you allow the fear of criticism, doubt and other people's negative suggestions to take shape in your mind, it will blot out the picture of your major purpose.

— *Napoleon Hill*

December 23

We must not ask where science and technology
are taking us, but rather how we can manage
science and technology so that they can help us
get where we want to go.

— *Rene Dubos*

The same law which holds our earth in its orbit
and relates it to all other planets in their orbits,
both in time and space, relates human beings to
one another in exact conformity with the nature
of their own thoughts.

— *Napoleon Hill*

December 24

Our impressions will become expressions just in
proportion to the vigor with which we register
our vows to accomplish our ambitions, to make
our visions realities.

— *Orison S. Marden*

When you speak of your ambitions, if at all,
use the past tense, after they have become
accomplishments and are not just words.

— *Napoleon Hill*

December 25

You nourish your soul by fulfilling your destiny,
by developing the potential that the soul represents.
— *Rabbi Harold Kushner*

Mental habits as well, including both poverty
consciousness and prosperity consciousness, are
fixed through the law of Cosmic Habitforce.
— *Napoleon Hill*

December 26

By failing to prepare you are preparing to fail.
— *Benjamin Franklin*

The stars and planets operate with clocklike
precision. They never collide, never get off their
appointed course, but roll on eternally, as the
result of a preconceived plan.
— *Napoleon Hill*

December 27

Nurture your mind with great thoughts, for you
will never go any higher than you think.
— *Benjamin Disraeli*

Let us repeat once more, for the sake of
emphasis: your mind acts like an
electro-magnet to attract to you the things upon
which you keep it focused.
— *Napoleon Hill*

December 28

The joy of life is in the journey. The fulfillment
of life is in the growing. Keep that growing
going, and never let it stop.
— *Ralph Marston*

The major distinguishing characteristic of
Cosmic Habitforce is that it forces all repeated
actions to become fixed habits, whether these
be the thoughts of a person or the orderly
movement of the stars or the coming and going
of the seasons.
— *Napoleon Hill*

December 29

I am not on this earth by chance. I am here for a purpose and that purpose is to grow into a mountain, not to shrink to a grain of sand. Henceforth will I apply all my effort to become the highest mountain of all, and I will strain my potential until it cries for mercy.

— *Og Mandino*

A strong will does not dwell on the past. A vital ego thrives on the hopes and desires of the yet unattained objective.

— *Napoleon Hill*

December 30

Plant the seed of desire in your mind and it forms a nucleus with power to attract to itself everything for its fulfillment.

— *Robert Collier*

You are where you are and what you are because of your established habits of thoughts and deeds.

— *Napoleon Hill*

December 31

Follow your bliss and don't be afraid,
and doors will open where you didn't
know they were going to be.

— *Joseph Campbell*

You now understand why the greatest of all riches
is a Positive Mental Attitude, for by means of such
an attitude it is possible to acquire all other things
which you may rightfully desire and possess.
What the mind can conceive and believe, it can
achieve with PMA!

— *Napoleon Hill*

NOTES

NOTES

NOTES